OHIO
JAZZ

OHIO
JAZZ

*A
History of*
JAZZ
*in the
Buckeye State*

DAVID MEYERS, CANDICE WATKINS,
ARNETT HOWARD & JAMES LOEFFLER

THE
History
PRESS

Published by The History Press

Charleston, SC 29403

www.historypress.net

Copyright © 2012 by David Meyers, Candice Watkins, Arnett Howard and James Loeffler

All rights reserved

First published 2012

Manufactured in the United States

ISBN 978.1.60949.575.6

Library of Congress CIP data applied for.

This book is dedicated to all Ohio musicians, especially those we didn't get to mention. We'll try to catch you next time! Till then, please—enjoy this book, share this book and send us more information about jazz artists in the great state of Ohio.

Contents

Forewords

I have a feeling, and it is confirmed by many in the New York jazz community where I now hang out, that there is something about the "heartland of Ohio" that makes one think of jazz as part of everyday life. Ohio has always been a great place to play jazz, hear jazz and learn jazz in a natural environment.

When I was a kid growing up in Columbus, Ohio, I somehow got interested in ragtime and Dixieland music. These old styles and forms of jazz somehow spoke to me and became the basis of a musical career. It never occurred to me that all this stuff was ancient and out of style, for in Columbus—and, indeed, all around Ohio—there were musicians, collectors of old records and fans who made it all come to life.

Columbus alone had at least six different clubs that featured Dixieland on any given night. But that was only part of our jazz world. I gradually learned that my hometown was home to a magnificent variety of jazz venues. It was indeed a big part of the cultural scene. Ray Eubanks's Jazz Arts Group attracted the who's who of the Columbus business community, as well as a wide range of us "just plain folks." Then there were the funky, old-time clubs on Columbus's East Side that often featured African American "recording star" musicians such as Rusty Bryant and Hank Marr. You could even hear world-class jazz concerts for free with your corn dogs and beer at the Ohio State Fair.

In more recent years, I've come to recognize that Ohio has a rich history of developing great jazz musicians. Beginning in the 1890s, when Cincinnati was home to several pioneers of ragtime composition, through the entire twentieth century, Ohio has continued to produce jazz masters. The impressive list includes such jazz legends as Cleveland Heights's Albert Ayler, who became a creator of "free form" jazz in the 1960s; Toledo's Art Tatum, who was possibly the greatest jazz piano player of all time; and Columbus's classic jazz vocalist Nancy Wilson.

This book finally tells the whole story (much of it, anyway) of Ohio's rich jazz heritage. I'm so pleased to be a part of it.

Terry Waldo, Musician and Historian
Author of *This Is Ragtime*

I think to be in love or married to a musician can be a tricky business. The fact is that on a bandstand there is a "life apart"; that is, a type of interaction and activity that can range from the very casual or informal to something bordering on a kind of intimacy. The "rules of engagement" vary from one band to another, but there is a version of a micro society on any bandstand.

The awareness or appreciation of this phenomenon on the part of the "significant other" can range from an uneasy sense that "something is going on" to a fully realized understanding and/or enjoyment of the world being witnessed.

Musicians generally enjoy first the music but then also the brotherhood or camaraderie they find themselves to be a part of. There is a sense of being unique or a "breed apart." No wonder, then, that musicians often compare their musical relationships to marriages. And, like many marriages, not all endure.

But it is sometimes good to be reminded of our past—even the heartbreaks—so, hopefully, we can learn from it. And I am especially glad there are people like David, Candy, Arnett and Jim who are willing to do the heavy lifting, swooping in after the breakup, retrieving the discarded love letters and castoff photos and sifting through the sometimes conflicting allegations of who did what, when and where to tell us the story—the true story of Ohio Jazz!

Vaughn Wiester, Director
Famous Jazz Orchestra

Acknowledgements

The genesis of this book was JazzOhio!—a unique partnership between the Ohio Historical Society and the Columbus-based Listen for the Jazz project, as well as many researchers and scholars from across the state. The exhibition featured photographs, recordings, musical instruments and other artifacts illustrating Ohio's rich and diverse jazz history. The intent of this volume is to capture and preserve these materials and additional Listen for the Jazz archives, lest they be lost to the dustbins of time.

In creating *Ohio Jazz: A History of Jazz in the Buckeye State*, the authors have plundered numerous books, articles, collections, memories and websites—too many to properly credit in such a slim volume. But several sources deserve special mention.

A graduate of Ohio University, Herman Leonard (1923–2010) moved to New York, where he opened his first studio in Greenwich Village. Driven by his love for jazz, he haunted the local clubs and photographed many of the musicians where he found them. Leonard kept his photos private until he staged his first exhibition in 1987, "Images of Jazz." These are marked ©Herman Leonard Photography LLC.

William P. Gottlieb (1917–2006) is widely known for his photographs from the Golden Age of American jazz, many of which appeared in *DownBeat*. His vast collection has been made available through the Library of Congress. They are marked WG-LOC.

Historian and photographer Duncan Schiedt has amassed one of the largest private collections of jazz images in the world and has very generously allowed the authors to use some of his treasures. They are marked DS.

Some of these images are from the authors' personal collections or the Listen for the Jazz archives. For simplicity's sake, they are all cited as LFTJ. Any other images are attributed to the individuals who contributed them to the extent possible.

Vaughn Wiester's foreword is adapted with permission from his foreword to Tennyson Williams's *Musical Moments in Jazz* (privately printed, 2011).

Finally, a special thanks to Lewis Williams Jr. for transcribing the original musician bios.

Introduction

All Americans come from Ohio originally, if only briefly.
—*Dawn Powell*

What we now call jazz (originally jas, jass or jasz) is an amalgamation of various non-jazz elements. Even the etymology of the word is a topic of ongoing debate. It first appeared in the early years of the twentieth century as a slang term referring to everything from sex to baseball before it finally became associated with this developing musical style.

While no one would dispute that New Orleans was the birthplace of jazz, the music itself is a heady gumbo in which bits of blues, spirituals, ragtime, hymns, brass band, minstrel, work songs and folk tunes can be seen (or, rather, heard) floating about in the rue. The ingredients may not have been unique to the Crescent City, but they were first mixed together there around 1895.

To paraphrase Len Weinstock,[1] it was the cross-pollination of the upper-class, often conservatory-trained Creole musicians with the generally uneducated, freed blacks of the "Back o' town" that first gave voice to this new way of playing. However, the city's white musicians weren't exactly standing on the sidelines; "Papa" Jack Laine's band frequently "blew out" its opponents in impromptu "battles" and spawned many other white ensembles.[2]

This intermarriage of marginalized cultures blended African rhythms and European harmony into a musical soundtrack that underscored life in Storyville, the city's legendary red-light district. When the Navy Department subsequently closed it down in 1917, many of the displaced musicians moved on, spreading their musical gospel. Historians have diligently tracked their migratory routes to Chicago, St. Louis, Kansas City, Detroit and New York.

As a consequence, the history of jazz tends to be viewed as the story of a few key cities. But this doesn't mean that jazz—good jazz—wasn't being played elsewhere. When he traveled the Midwest with his father at the turn of the century, trombonist Wilber DeParis (born in 1900) told Leonard Feather he had heard numerous bands playing jazz. "Jazz," he said, "was developing all over America"—Ohio included.

Most histories of jazz give short shrift to Ohio, but a geography of jazz would be hard pressed to ignore it. Many important musicians got their start in Ohio, many important venues were located in Ohio and many important events in jazz history occurred in Ohio. Owing to its strategic location (especially in those pre–"flyover country" days) and its high population density, Ohio was—and is—a major jazz state.

In *Music in Ohio*, William Osborne acknowledges that "jazz has been practiced in Ohio and with a vengeance."[3] He echoes the often heard view that Ohio was considered by most of the jazz world as a "go through" rather than a "go to" place. But in going through, the musicians left some influences behind while taking others with them, contributing to the state's rich musical heritage.

Ohio has become home to some of the best music schools and jazz studies programs to be found anywhere. The sheer number of musicians who have passed through the state's many institutions of higher learning is staggering. And even more Ohio sons and daughters have passed through what is fondly called "Nightclub U" (university).

What would jazz piano be like without Toledo's Art Tatum? Where would Duke Ellington have been without longtime collaborator Billy Strayhorn from Dayton? Imagine the development of jazz singing without the contribution of vocalese exponent Jon Hendricks of Newark. Has there ever been a better vibraphone player than Springfield's Johnny Lytle? And who can compare to the incomparable Rahsaan Roland Kirk from Columbus?

Art Ryerson, Harry "Sweets" Edison and Bobby Byrne all worked together at one time or another, without ever realizing they shared the same hometown.[4] When they met for the first time in a New York City recording studio, the question of "What's your hometown?" apparently never came up. Each was a highly respected figure in the jazz field. Each had taken a different path to the upper ranks of his profession. And each traced his roots back to Ohio.[5]

Thomas Carlyle said, "The history of the world is but the biography of great men." If you subscribe to the great man/person theory of history, you will find in the last chapter brief biographies (noted by the symbol ♪)

of sixty Ohioans who significantly contributed to the development of jazz. However, if you are more inclined to the every man/person theory, you will see numerous examples of how jazz evolved through the cumulative efforts of the many, including many Buckeyes.

When Von Freeman of Chicago was named an NEA Jazz Master in 2011, Geoffrey Hines wrote,

> *it meant more than the recognition of another saxophonist. The announcement also rekindled an argument about jazz history: Should we focus only on the artists who developed a national reputation? Or should the narrative also include those artists who stayed hunkered down in their hometowns to stay close to their families, devote themselves to the local scene and hone their craft? If those players attained technical mastery and distinctively original voices, shouldn't they too find a place in history books?*[26]

You are holding the answer to that question in your hands. For thirty years, the authors have been researching and documenting the history of music, particularly jazz, in Ohio. The 1999 exhibition at the Ohio Historical Society, JazzOhio!, ran for twelve months before portions of it moved to the Rock and Roll Hall of Fame for use in the Roots of Rock & Roll Exhibition. *Ohio Jazz: A History of Jazz in the Buckeye State* is built on the materials gathered for that exhibition. Much of what you will read here has never been brought together in one place before—and it may well change the way you think about jazz. And Ohio.

David Meyers
Candice Watkins

1

Before It Even Had a Name

Ragtime is not jazz, but any discussion of early jazz begins with ragtime. The musicians who first played what is now considered jazz did not call it that for many years. In fact, they didn't call it anything. Sidney Bechet, the first important jazz soloist on record, always insisted that jazz was "a name the white people have given to the music." To him, it was all ragtime.

Regarded as the first wholly American musical genre,[7] ragtime may have been named for its syncopated or "ragged movement," which made it popular for dancing. It has also been suggested that it refers to signaling the start of a dance by holding up a bandana or rag as if to say, "It's rag time."

Ragtime was first heard in the brothels of New Orleans, Kansas City, St. Louis and other cities of the largely southern Midwest sometime during the 1890s. According to Albert McCarthy, the development of syncopation—the essence of ragtime—was "the most outstanding characteristics of popular music during 1890 and 1910."[8] In their simplest form, rags were marches with the accent on the "off" beats.

While Scott Joplin is one of the few ragtime composers who still enjoys a measure of name recognition, he was neither the first nor, some believe, the best. The self-proclaimed "King of Ragtime Writers," he quickly grew to dislike the term, believing it detracted from the dignity and grace of the music. He always insisted, "It is never right to play ragtime fast."

Joplin has rightfully been called the "Father of Ragtime Music," but so have Benjamin Robertson Harney, Ernest Hogan, Ferdinand "Jelly Roll" Morton and a few others, including Shepard N. Edmonds (1876–1957) of Columbus.[9]

According to Sylvester Russell,[10] Edmonds "came very near to jubilee in his rag-time compositions"—that is to say, he approached perfection. A well-

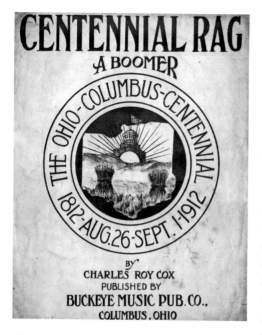

Charles Roy Cox was a championship horseshoe pitcher, pulp fiction writer and, for a time, composer and music publisher. *LFTJ.*

known musician and something of a "show off,"[11] Edmonds left home with the Al G. Field Minstrels in 1895. It wasn't long before Edmonds was writing songs as well as performing.

With the money he earned from "I'm Going to Live Anyhow Until I Die" (1901), Edmonds established the Attucks Music Publishing Company in 1903, the first African American–owned music publishing concern in New York City. It was anything but a vanity press. Edmonds did not publish a single one of his own songs. Instead, he sought out the most talented tunesmiths he could find and quickly scored a major hit with Bert Williams's signature song, "Nobody" (1905).

Edmonds claimed he sold his small firm for $55,000 (more than $1 million in today's dollars) to Will Marion Cook and Richard C. McPherson, who merged it with their own Gotham Music Company. Cook had Ohio ties as well, having studied violin at Oberlin College Conservatory (his mother's alma mater). Because Gotham-Attucks had an even stronger stable of songwriting talent (and the genius of Cook), it came to overshadow Edmonds's pioneering achievements. He was subsequently forced to sue Gotham-Attucks and other publishers for uncollected song royalties before going on to found Edmonds National Detective Bureau in 1907.

Roy Carew [12] thought Edmonds had written over two thousand songs, but "fewer than thirty" (the number is actually closer to forty) were ever published. Just prior to World War II, Edmonds retired to Columbus, where author Rudi Blesh "rediscovered" him and probed his memory for his book *They All Played Ragtime.*

Whether William Krell's "The Mississippi Rag" (1897) or Theodore H. Northrup's "The Louisiana Rag" (1897) was the first published rag is still debated by scholars (with some insisting the former is actually a cakewalk). The same year, however, a little-known songwriter in Cincinnati, Robert S. "Bob" Roberts (1879–1930), published "The Pride of Bucktown" and "A Bundle of Rags," both of which are said to alternate between cakewalk rhythmic patterns and syncopated piano figures. Sometimes known as "Ragtime" Roberts, he began a prolific recording career in 1902. His biggest hit was "He Walked Right In, Turned Around and Walked Right Out Again" (1906), but he also did well with "Ragtime Cowboy Joe" (1912). After moving to New York's Tin Pan Alley, Roberts collaborated with Gene Jefferson on "I'm Certainly Living a Ragtime Life" (1900).

According to Shep Edmonds, the cakewalk was "originally a plantation dance, just a happy movement." The rag combines the structure of a march with the polyrhythms of African American dance tunes. It's just a matter of where you draw the line.

A conservatory-trained bandleader in Columbus named Frederick L. Neddermeyer (1866–1924) was the first person to publish a tune

One of composer and bandleader Fred Neddermeyer's various ensembles. *American Federation of Musicians–Local 103.*

that approximated the cakewalk style. According to David A. Jasen,[13] Neddermeyer's "Happy Hottentots" (1889) was the "true" predecessor to the cakewalk.[14] Three years later, his "Opelika Cake Walk" was the first self-proclaimed cakewalk, although an actual cakewalk wasn't published until 1895. Neddermeyer also wrote occasional rags, such as "In Colored Circles: A Ragtime Rhapsody" (1898), and other pieces that straddle the line between rags and cakewalks. The same year, Will Marion Cook and famed Dayton poet Paul Lawrence Dunbar collaborated on *Clorindy, The Origin of the Cakewalk*.

Cincinnati was a major printing and publishing center from its earliest days. Not surprisingly, it was quick to develop into a hotbed of ragtime composers and home to numerous publishing houses, ranking fourth behind New York, Chicago and St. Louis. It has been estimated that more than 110 ragtime compositions were published in Cincinnati by Miller-Arnold, Great Eastern Publishing Co., the Groene Music Publishing Co., Joseph Krolage Music Publishing Co., Mentel Bros. Publishing Co. and others.[15]

Originally from Kentucky, Louis H. Mentel (1881–unknown) was a musician, music publisher and operator of a roadhouse outside Cincinnati. He also authored a number of rags, including "Lagoon Breeze" (1903), "Gasoline Rag" (1906) and "Bunch of Noise Rag" (1908).

"The Amazon Rag" (1904), by Cincinnati violinist Teddy Hahn (1882–1961), was praised as an example of "the adventuresome ragtime tastes of Cincinnati publisher John Arnold."[16] His use of broken-chord phrasing would later be incorporated into many novelty tunes.

Pianist and composer Dr. Artie Matthews (1888–1958) spent his early adulthood in the ragtime cities of St. Louis and Chicago, soaking up influences.[17] In 1913, publisher John Stark offered Matthews fifty dollars for every original rag he composed. Three years later, Matthews moved to Cincinnati to take a job as a church organist. In 1921, he and his wife founded the Cosmopolitan School of Music in the city's west end, the first African American–owned and operated music conservatory in the country. Among its students was future Count Basie arranger Frank Foster, whose mother was an instructor.

In the annals of ragtime, Matthews's compositions are regarded as some of the most sophisticated, rivaling those of Scott Joplin, Joseph Lamb, Tom Turpin and other masters. His most famous rags are the five "Pastime Rags" (1913–1920). He also arranged and published "Baby Seal's Blues" (written by Arthur F. "Baby" Seales) in 1912, the same year W.C. Handy came out with "Memphis Blues." However, his best-known composition is the Dixieland standard "Weary Blues" (1915).

The longtime calliope player on the *Island Queen* steamer, Homer Denney (1885–1975) may have been the best-known musician in the Queen City. Originally from Gallipolis, he wrote a dozen or so first-rate rags, including "No Ze" (1905), "Hot Cabbage" (1908) "and "Chimes" (1910).

After moving to Cincinnati with his parents in the 1890s, Albert Gumble (1883–1946) studied with Clarence Adler (whose students included composers Aaron Copland and Richard Rodgers). His self-published "Bolo Rag" (1907) landed him a job with the New York publishing house of Jerome Remick. Other rags soon followed: "The Georgia Rag" (1910), "Chanticleer Rag" (1910) and "Red Rose Rag" (1911).

Self-taught musician Joe Jordan (1882–1971) was born in Cincinnati, attended college in Missouri and started working in the cafés and brothels of St. Louis before eventually settling in Chicago. He is credited with more than six hundred songs. After the Original Dixieland Jass Band became the first group to record a jazz tune, "Livery Stable Blues," in 1917, Jordan was able to establish in court that the trio section of the band's "Original Dixieland Jazz Band One Step" had been lifted intact from his own composition, "That Teasin' Rag" (1909).

Cincinnati son Abraham Olshewitz, aka Abe Olman (1887/8–1984), was a renowned songwriter and composer. In addition to writing a number of pop hits (including "O-HI-O (O-My!-O!)"), he authored a half dozen rags such as "Honeymoon Rag" (1908), "Candle Stick Rig" (1910) and, his most famous, "Red Onion Rag" (1912).

Harry P. Guy (1870–1950) was born in Zanesville and published his first song at the age of seventeen while working as the accompanist for the Cincinnati Opera Club. It wasn't until he was twenty-five that he settled in Detroit, where he came to be regarded as one of the city's "unique and unusually gifted musicians." Many ragtime musicians traveled to Detroit specifically to play with Guy (who was a member of the Finney Orchestra, founded by Theodore Finney, formerly of Columbus). One of Guy's most celebrated rags, "Echoes of the Snowball Club" (1898), remains in print.

Of course, not all of Ohio's ragtime composers have Cincinnati ties. Clarence M. Jones (1889–1949) was born in Wilmington[18] and learned piano from his mother. By 1910, he was performing in Chicago, where he crossed paths with Jelly Roll Morton. Best known for his prowess as a boogie-woogie piano player and piano-roll artist, he composed "Wild Grapes Rag" (1910), "That Baseball Rag" (1912) and "Modulations" (1923). In 1922, Clarence M. Jones and His Wonder Orchestra was the first African American dance band to broadcast over Chicago radio.

Hailing from the village of Blue Earth in Adams County, Clarence H. Woods (1888–1956) learned piano in Carthage, Missouri, before working the vaudeville circuit in Texas and Oklahoma. Dubbed the "Ragtime Wonder of the South" for his skill as a performer, Woods also wrote a handful of rags such as "Slippery Elm Rag" (1912) and "Sleepy Hollow Rag" (1918).

Roy Frederick Bargy (1894–1974) grew up in Toledo, where he accompanied films in the local silent movie theaters. Moving to Chicago in his early twenties, he was working as an editor of piano rolls while composing many fine rags such as "Ruffenreddy" (1921), "Slipova" (1921) and "Knice and Knifty" (1922). In the 1929 Hollywood biography of Whiteman, *King of Jazz*, Bargy demonstrated his keyboard virtuosity on Gershwin's "Rhapsody in Blue."

Cleveland was home to several important ragtime publishers, primarily Sam Fox but also Fred Heltman Co. and Popular Music. Fred Dunhill Heltman (1867–1960) was one of the city's top ragtime composers. Among his tunes were "Daisy Rag" (1909), "Chewin' the Rag" (1913) and "Fred Heltman's Rag" (1918).

Women also composed ragtime songs. Elsie Janis (1889–1956), born Elsie Bierbower in Columbus, was a child star in vaudeville and on Broadway prior to World War I. Between 1912 and 1919, she recorded several ragtime and early jazz-tinged songs (ranging from her own "Fo' de Lawd's Sake Play a Waltz" to "Darktown Strutters' Ball"), both in the United States and Britain. Although one of her compositions was the tongue-in-cheek "Anti Rag-Time Girl" (1913), Janis was open to all styles of music.

Ragtime had taken the country by storm. Schools of Syncopation were opening in storefronts all across the country. In 1910, Harry Click offered to teach anyone how to play one song for free at his Awanda Music Studio in Cincinnati. Rags became so popular that the *Cleveland Plain Dealer* reported in 1914 that a horse had "foxtrotted" across a sidewalk dragging a Wells Fargo Express wagon behind it after it heard a popular ragtime tune emanating from a phonograph.

John Philip Sousa, the most popular bandleader of his generation, had enthusiastically incorporated ragtime arrangements into his concerts as "an established feature of American Music." But in 1909, he declared it dead. "Ragtime had the dyspepsia or the gout long before it died," he was quoted as saying in the *New York Times*. "It was overfed by poor nurses. Good ragtime came, and half a million imitators sprang up. Then, as a result, the people were sickened with the stuff. I have not played a single piece of ragtime this season, and it is simply because the people do not want it."

She wasn't really anti-ragtime, but Elsie Janis spoofed the new dances in her song "Anti Rag-Time Girl" (1913). *LFTJ.*

However, the country wasn't quite finished with rags (and probably never will be). And not a few of those written by Ohio composers still remain in print a century later. When asked to define the term in 1920, Dayton musician George Booher said, "Rags make paper, paper makes money, money makes banks, banks make loans, loans make poverty, poverty makes rags."[19]

2
The Jazz Diaspora

Even though the-thing-we-now-call-jazz was born in New Orleans—roughly eight hundred miles southwest of Cincinnati—it wasn't long before there were pockets of jazz springing up all over the country. Recording[20] was in its infancy, and radio existed only in a few isolated laboratories. So how was this new style of music transmitted? What routes did it travel? Who were the carriers?

The Jazz Diaspora refers primarily to the migration of early African American jazz musicians to other parts of the country and even abroad. Many artists who went to Britain, France, Holland and elsewhere wound up staying because they were often better received. While at home jazz had to overcome its humble beginnings (not to mention Jim Crow laws), in Europe the music and its acolytes were often embraced as the latest in high culture.

Musicians are nomadic by nature, always going where the jobs are. A few historians have even suggested that New Orleans–style jazz spread by riverboat to Chicago (where it was given its own twist) via the Mississippi River, apparently unaware that the Mississippi, even at its wildest, veers far left of the Windy City. However, the riverboat does play an important role in the process, as do brass bands, circuses, minstrel shows, vaudeville and other popular entertainments.

Headquartered in Columbus, Al G. Field Greater Minstrels billed itself as the "Oldest, Biggest and Best Minstrel Show in the World." Field's troupe had been crisscrossing the nation and, occasionally, the oceans since 1886. It was an incubator for some of the best musical talent in the country, many of whom would figure in the development of vaudeville and the early recording industry (including the nation's first recording star, William Thomas "Billy" Murray). It also helped to introduce the public to ragtime and early jazz.

Just before his death, Mount Vernon–native Daniel Decatur Emmett (1815–1904) was lured out of retirement by Al Field for one more season. At the age of fifteen, Emmett had already written "Old Dan Tucker" (1830). He later composed "Dixie" (circa 1850), the song that would later lend its name to a specific type of jazz: Dixieland. Emmett had originated the concept of the minstrel show in 1843, when he formed the Virginny Minstrels. After a year in the army, during which he witnessed slavery for the first time in Kentucky and Missouri, he returned to Ohio and began writing fanciful songs of plantation life. By 1840, he was "corking up" (covering his face with burnt cork) and performing songs in imitation of the slaves and ex-slaves he had encountered in his travels.

Minstrel music was another ingredient in the jazz gumbo. And Scott Joplin was one of many ragtime performers who had worked in minstrel shows.

Not long afterward, Stephen Foster (1826–1864) came to Cincinnati to take a job with his brother's steamboat company. He soon began writing the songs that would make him famous, inspired by the folk tunes of the African American laborers who lived and worked on the Ohio riverfront. Songs such as "Oh, Susanna!" (1848) and "Camptown Races" (1850), both from this period, as well as "Old Folks at Home (Swanee River)" (1851) and "My Old Kentucky Home" (1853) became staples of minstrel shows.

When Westerville's Benjamin Hanby (1833–1867) wrote "Darling Nelly Gray" (1855–56), it rapidly became the most popular song of the nineteenth century next to Foster's "Old Folks at Home." Together, Hanby and Foster—one an Ohio native and the other an Ohio resident—practically invented American popular song.

Showman P.T. Barnum, who had originally transported his circus throughout the country on steamships and canal boats, helped pioneer the first circus train in 1872. Circus bands offered work to first-rate musicians and developed loyal followings, especially in African American communities. Trumpeters Willie "Bunk" Johnson, Roy Eldridge and Harry James all got their starts in circus bands. Drummer William McKinney and clarinet pioneer Wilbur C. Sweatman[21] were also veteran circus musicians. "These bands," Thomas J. Hennessey wrote, "demanded a complex repertoire; marches in the parade to signal the show's arrival in town; marches and overtures in concerts on the midway; and overtures, instrumental ragtime, and popular music to back up the sideshow acts. Often, after-hours, they were playing ragtime and blues for local dances."[22]

During this era, it wasn't uncommon for circuses to travel with two bands; an all-white ensemble would play for the big top while an all-black one handled the sideshow. Since management's focus was on the main attraction, the sideshow musicians were free to incorporate blues, ragtime and, ultimately, jazz into their repertoires. And as the circuses traveled from town to town, the new musical sounds gained exposure. Elvin Jones was inspired to take up the drums after watching a drummer in a circus band.

In 1989, Boston Conservatory graduate Perry George Lowery (1869–1942) was reputed to be one of the country's best cornetists when he was hired to run the band and "annex" for the Columbus-based Forepaugh-Sells Brothers Circus. Lowery expanded the circus band from ten to twenty-three pieces and introduced ragtime music. He is credited with being the first band director to create sideshow entertainment in circuses, combining bands and minstrels in vaudeville performances. In 1920, Lowery, by this time with the Ringling Brothers Barnum & Bailey sideshow, led one of the hottest jazz bands in the country, playing "everything from ragtime to opera…jazz to overtures."[23]

Marches also figured in the development of ragtime. While John Philip Sousa, the "March King," did more to popularize the march than anyone else, both James Henry Fillmore Jr. (1881–1956) of Cincinnati and Karl L. King (1891–1971) of Paintersville composed hundreds of marches, many of them nearly as well known.

Karl King got his start as a teenager in Neddermeyer's band and later wrote "Neddermeyer's Triumphal March" (1911) to honor his mentor. He also played baritone horn with the John Robinson, Yankee Robinson, Sells-Floto and Barnum & Bailey Circus bands. In addition to composing Barnum and Bailey's "Favorite" (1913), he penned other marches and two-steps that had elements of ragtime such as "Ragged Rosey" (1913), "Kentucky Sunrise" (1919) and "The Walking Frog" (1919).

While traveling the country as a circus bandmaster, James Henry Fillmore became famous as the "Father of the Trombone Smear." He wrote a total of fifteen "smears" from 1908 to 1929, with such titles as "Miss Trombone" (1911), "Sally Trombone" (1917) and "Bull Trombone" (1924), all of which had a ragtime flavor.

Lawrence Gushee has made the argument that the Original Creole Band was the first true jazz band to carry the sound of New Orleans to the rest of America. However, when the band toured Canada in 1916, the *Manitoba Free Press* reported "the music is weird reminding one of an old circus band."[24]

Following in Sousa's wake, community brass bands became ubiquitous during the late nineteenth and early twentieth centuries, fueled by the widespread availability of brass instruments after the Civil War. These organizations sought to outdo one another by inserting classical pieces, popular songs and other new musical ideas into their standard repertoire of marches. Civic pride was embodied in these ensembles and intense rivalries developed, especially between neighboring towns.

While living in Columbus, Percy George Lowery also took over leadership of the Ninth Ohio National Guard Concert Band. It was already a crowded field. The 1900 Columbus city directory listed eight such musical organizations. Within four years, two more had also come into being. Others representing various fraternal groups, military companies and businesses were also known to be active.

When young Theodore Friedman ran away from his Circleville home, he joined the band of a traveling carnival. Working his way up through county fairs and vaudeville theaters, he arrived in New York City, where he landed in Earl Fuller's Famous Jazz Band. Signed to the Victor label, Fuller and his boys were possibly the first recording group ever promoted as "hot."[25]

Once ranked as one the five greatest showmen of all time (along with Enrico Caruso, Will Rogers, Charlie Chaplin and John Barrymore), Ted

By 1917, Ted Lewis (arm behind head) was already the star of Earl Fuller's Famous Jazz Band, and within a few years, he was one of the biggest stars in the world. *DS.*

Lewis', as Friedman was better known, soon put together an orchestra that ranked as one of the finest of the era and included such future stars as Muggsy Spanier, Benny Goodman, Jimmy Dorsey and Fats Waller. He is at his best on such recordings as "Dip Your Brush in the Sunshine" (1929).

By the time Louis Armstrong signed up to play with Fate C. Marable's dance band aboard the steamer *Sidney* in 1919, riverboat traffic on the Mississippi and Ohio Rivers had been providing musicians with steady employment for a couple of decades. Not surprisingly, these floating dance halls (more than one hundred of them) became a vehicle for spreading new musical ideas throughout the Midwest and the South. The river towns of Memphis, St. Louis, Louisville and Cincinnati were linked together like charms on a bracelet.

In 1960, Verne Streckfus, owner of the Streckfus Steamer Company, insisted that "the dancers on the *Sidney* liked 'straight' music—fox trots, waltzes, and one-steps. The bands played stock arrangements, music as it was published, not distorted by arrangements." Still, whatever they played, they must have played it well, for in addition to Armstrong, other notable riverboat musicians were Leon "Bix" Beiderbecke, Clark Terry and Henry "Red" Allen. And for many years, "riverboat jazz" was considered the only authentic variety.

Composer George Russell recalled, "[In] my neighborhood [was] Zack Whyte, one of the first people to have a band on a riverboat that went from Cincinnati up the Ohio to St. Louis and then down to New Orleans. It was bands like that that really began to get to me. They were really attractive and the music was attractive."[26]

In the early 1920s, banjo player Zack Whyte' attended Wilberforce College, where he was an early member of Horace Henderson's Collegians. By 1925, he had organized his own Cincinnati-based band, the Chocolate Beau Brummels. Considered one of the first territory bands because it worked in a particular geographic region rather than a major East Coast city, the band played wherever it was wanted, including on riverboats. At various times, Whyte could boast such stellar musicians as Vic Dickenson, Herman Chittison and Al Sears.

Whyte's band had been using "head arrangements" with the harmonies doled out by music director "Smoke" Richardson. But the key to the band's sound became the innovative arrangements by Sy Oliver', who preferred writing to playing the trumpet. The development of written arrangements was an important event in the evolution of dance bands, and Oliver was clearly in the forefront.

After three years with Whyte, Oliver was hired by Alphonso Trent to write a new "book" of arrangements for his band because it had lost its book in a Cleveland fire. But when Trent became seriously ill while on tour in 1933, the band broke up in Columbus, Ohio (another source says Albany, New York). Two members of the sax section, James Jeter and Hayes Pillars, childhood friends, decided to form their own band, and not a few of Trent's musicians followed them.

Trumpeter Harry "Sweets" Edison♪ was only eighteen years old when he joined the Jeter-Pillars Orchestra, along with reedman Norris Turney♪. Arrangers for the band included Ernie Wilkins, who also got his start at Wilberforce, and Tadd Dameron♪, who created his first big band arrangement for them: "I Let a Song Go Out of My Heart." The band eventually moved from Cleveland to Chicago and then down to

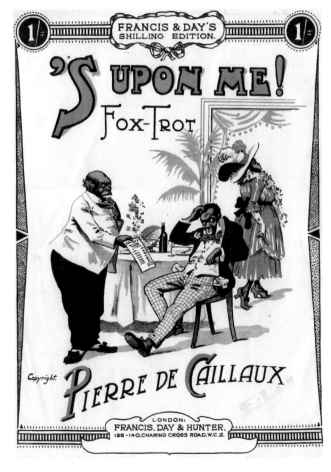

In 1921, Pierre de Caillaux (aka Lionel Jones) might have participated in the first recording of a jazz soloist, Sidney Bechet, just a year after he published this song. *LFTJ.*

29

St. Louis—performing on a riverboat—before breaking up in 1947. However, by then most bands were traveling by train, bus and automobile. And most of them crisscrossed Ohio—repeatedly.

For some Ohio musicians, though, even these modes of transportation were inadequate; they were among the first musicians to carry jazz overseas, traveling by steamship. In 1919, Will Marion Cook's Southern Syncopated Orchestra toured Europe. This large ensemble (twenty-seven musicians, nineteen singers) included the first important jazz soloist, clarinetist Sidney Bechet, and a piano player who called himself Pierre de Caillaux (1897–1956) but was known as Lionel Jones in his hometown of Columbus.

After hearing Cook's orchestra in concert, a Swiss writer, Ernest Alexandre-Ansermet, wrote what is considered the first serious review of a jazz group: "They play generally without written music, and even when they have it, the score only serves to indicate the general line, for there are very few numbers I have heard them execute twice with exactly the same effects."

Two years later, Bechet and Caillaux entered a London studio and recorded for the first time as Benny Payton's Jazz Kings. Sadly, the recordings were never issued due to technical problems. Instead, it would be a couple more years before a true jazz solo—by Bechet—was captured on record. But by then, jazz had already spread as far away as China, where Clinton Mooreman, a banjo and guitar player from Columbus, was performing in a Shanghai hotel.

3

The Coming of the
Jazz Age

Ragtime was dance music, but it had an image problem. Born in brothels, juke joints and dance halls, it featured provocative movements that were considered naughty, if not downright obscene, by polite society. That changed in 1914, when Vernon and Irene Castle made a whirlwind tour of the United States, playing thirty cities in twenty-eight days.

The Castles—one a British entertainer, the other the daughter of an American doctor—quickly taught the rest of the country how to dance. Irene later recalled the basis of their appeal: "We were clean-cut, we were married, and when we danced there was nothing suggestive about it." They were pioneers in other respects, too. The ten-piece band that accompanied them was composed entirely of African American musicians, led by the remarkable James Reese Europe.

Americans had wanted to dance for a long time. A dancing school opened in Cincinnati in 1799, a mere eleven years after the arrival of the first settlers.[27] Between 1912 and 1914, "over one hundred new dances found their way, in and out of our fashionable ballrooms."[28]

By the age of twenty-three, William J. Rader of Columbus, son of a prominent farmer, had established himself as the most proficient teacher of dancing in the capital city. In 1898, he founded the Professor W.H. Rader Academies of Dance, possibly the first franchised dancing schools (Arthur Murray didn't start his own until 1925).[29] Rader insisted, "The exercise of dancing is not only conducive to health when properly taught, but is equally efficacious in promoting physical development."

By the time the Castles brought their act to Ohio, they found that the state of dance in the Buckeye state was not to their liking. The problem, as

Irene put it, was "the farther we come from New York, the more exaggerated seems to be the dancing. The dip, bend and kick went out a year ago. What we teach is simple, graceful dancing."[30]

Dancing was a very important form of recreation, not just in Ohio, but also across the entire Midwest. Virtually every community in the state had a venue of some sort where dances were held. As a result, the demand for dance bands playing the new syncopated style was enormous. Biographer Edward Jablonski believes there were more than sixty thousand dance bands across the nation at the beginning of the 1920s.

Charles A. Parker, an African American barber and violinist from Columbus, managed as many as thirty-eight bands throughout the Midwest. Billed as "Comedians with Rag Time Orchestra," Parker's Popular Players played everything from "tea music" to "jass." His biggest competitor was Thomas "Tom" Howard, a Columbus restaurant owner. Howard handled such groups as the People's Orchestra, the Orchestra Deluxe and the Whispering Orchestra of Gold.

Both Parker and Howard benefitted from Columbus's proximity to the large populations of Cleveland, Toledo and Detroit when it came to booking one-nighters. While all of those cities had capable groups of their own, competition was keen, and bands frequently invaded one another's territory.

Parker's Popular Players was one of thirty-eight bands managed by barber and violinist Charles A. Parker in the early 1900s. *LFTJ.*

Sammy Stewart*, a pianist and arranger, left Parker's Popular Players in 1918 to form his own band, Sammy Stewart's Singing Syncopators (later known as the Ten Knights of Syncopation). Some of Parker's best men joined him. According to his *New York Times* obituary, Stewart was one of the first midwestern conductors to use Paul Whiteman–style symphonic jazz arrangements. He was also credited with introducing choral singing by members of the orchestra. However, his greatest accomplishment was when he took his band to Chicago in 1923 and quickly established it as one of the top five in the city, effectively breaking free of the territory band niche.

A year later, Stewart took his orchestra to Paramount Studios to record "My Man Rocks Me," "Manda" and "Copenhagen" in the symphonic jazz style that had won over the Windy City. Four more years passed before they recorded again, but the formula was the same. In between, however, Dixon's Jazz Maniacs, a trio of Stewart's musicians (banjoist Lawrence Dixon, reed player Vance Dixon and pianist Kline Tyndall), showed they could also play "hot" when they had the chance, cutting loose on "D A D Blues," "Tiger Rag," "Crazy Quilt" and "My Man Just Won't Don't."

Another veteran of Parker's Popular Players, violinist Earl Hood stayed behind to organize his own Columbus dance band. Had he chosen to go the "territory" route, there is no question he could have been successful. However, Hood had a good day job with the county auditor's office and did not want to give it up. Instead, the Earl Hood Orchestra settled in as the house band at Valley Dale Ballroom and served as an important training ground for many future stars, most notably Harry "Sweets" Edison*, Melvin "Sy" Oliver* and Lawrence Dixon*.

During its era, this band was acknowledged as the gold standard in Columbus, and Hood insisted he had no local competition—with the exception of "Skin Young's Band."

Austin "Skin" Young was a Columbus singer who also played guitar and banjo. Picked up by Paul Whiteman after a stint with the Mason-Dixon Orchestra, he was soon pulling down one of the largest paychecks in the band—a band that included such heavy hitters as Bix Beiderbecke, Jimmy Dorsey, Tommy Dorsey and Frankie Trumbauer.

However, another group was also winning fans in Columbus. A regular attraction at Olentangy Park's Moonlight Gardens, Eddie Mitchell's Orchestra was, according to an article in the *Ohio State Journal*, "a musical organization rated as one of the best of its kind in the country." A couple of lively tunes recorded at Gennett Studios in 1925, "Pleasure Mad" and "Pickin' 'Em Up," include an accordion break!

The National Amusement Corporation of Detroit presents

McKINNEY'S
[ORIGINAL]
COTTON PICKERS
VICTOR RECORD ARTISTS
AMERICA'S GREATEST COLORED ORCHESTRA

CLYFFESIDE CASINO
ASHLAND, KY.
OCTOBER 19th
Dancing 9-2   Subscription $2.00 per Couple

Sponsored by Oscar Youngdale

A 1930 poster of McKinney's Cotton Pickers: Todd Rhodes, Dave Wilborn, Cuba Austin, Don Redman, Ralph Escudero, George Thomas, Prince Robinson, Jimmy Dudley, Joe Smith (Ripley), John Nesbit, Milton Senior and William McKinney. *LFTJ.*

Less than fifty miles away in Springfield, Kentucky-born William McKinney, a former circus drummer, joined the Synco Septet (later Synco Jazz Band) around 1920. Three years later, he quit the drums in order to concentrate on managing the band. After relocating to Detroit in 1926, McKinney expanded the group to ten pieces and renamed it McKinney's Cotton Pickers. With arrangements by Benny Carter and others, the band's fame spread far beyond the bounds of a typical territory band.

In 1922, the Scott brothers' (Cecil on reeds and Lloyd on drums) formed their own Springfield-area band, Scott's Symphonic Syncopators, to compete with McKinney's group. Soon, Lloyd gave up drumming to become the Syncopators' manager. Renamed Cecil Scott and His Bright Boys, the band was known for its hot arrangements and hot musicians, particularly trombonist Dickey Wells and trumpeter Bill Coleman. By 1929, the ten-piece ensemble was operating out of Harlem, where it remained active into the early 1930s.

About the same time, Springfield native Lois Deppe' formed a band in Pittsburgh with a teenage pianist, Earl Hines. Calling themselves Deppe's Serenaders, they made a pilgrimage to Richmond, Indiana, in October and November 1923 to record six tunes, including "Sometimes I Feel Like a Motherless Child," "Dear Old Southland" and "Congaine." Sammy Stewart wound up taking several of Deppe's musicians (including Hines) for his own group.

Lois Deppe's Serenaders, with Earl Hines (center) and Lois Deppe (above the drum). *DS.*

Saxophonist Milton "Milt" Senior, an original member of the Synco Septet (and the earlier Willis-Warmack-Willis Trio out of Dayton), moved 130 miles north to Toledo, where he started the Milt Senior Synco Septet and a few other combos. Finding it difficult to compete with the bands coming out of Detroit, Senior became one of the region's most prominent booking agents instead. A good eye for talent, he hired a teenage Art Tatum* for one of his bands. When the young pianist left a year later, Senior quickly replaced him with somebody almost as good, Theodore "Teddy" Wilson.

One of the most prominent bandleaders in northwest Ohio was Piqua's Harold Greenamyer (1899–1982). In 1922, Greenamyer hired a seventeen-year-old cornet player from Ogden, Utah, named Ernest Loring "Red" Nichols. (Nichols remained with the band for a couple months before continuing his climb to fame and fortune with his own group, the Five Pennies.) Greenamyer's band also included drummer "Humpty" Horlocker, who is credited with making the first drum sticks when the Rogers Drum Company in Covington (twenty-five miles north of Dayton) got its first stick machine.

The fact that many banjo players became bandleaders reflects the importance of the instrument in the development of syncopated rhythms.

Scott's Symphonic Syncopators (from Springfield) included, *from left to right*: Earl Horne (trombone), Gus McClung (trumpet), Buddy Burdton (violin), Dave Wilborn (banjo), Lloyd Scott (drums), Don Frye (piano) and Cecil Scott (reeds). *DS.*

Marion McKay, possibly from Indiana, led a territory band that made the rounds throughout Cincinnati, Detroit and Cleveland, with occasional side trips to New York and California. His brother, Ernie, on clarinet and sax, and pianist Henry Lange were also members of the group. Marion McKay and His Orchestra cut numerous sides for Gennett, including "Doo-Wacka-Doo" (1924).[31] In 1927, when they were playing at Castle Farms near Cincinnati, they switched places with Jean Goldkette's Orchestra in Detroit.

Henry W. Lange (1896–1985), once billed as the "Monarch of the Ivories," was inspired to become a musician after attending a concert by his hometown Toledo Orchestra. As a member of the Paul Whiteman Orchestra, he was one of a trio of pianists, along with composer George Gershwin and arranger Ferde Grofe, for the premiere performance of "Rhapsody in Blue" in 1924. The same year, he took over Marion McKay's band and renamed it the Lange-McKay Orchestra. They cut three tracks for Gennett: "Sweet Little You," "Tea For Two" and "Leaky Roof Blues."

Despite the name, J. Frank Terry's Chicago Nightingales was a Toledo-based band that got its start in the mid-1920s and, undoubtedly, gave Milt Senior a run for his money. Apparently, Terry believed that having "Chicago" in the band's name would make it more bookable. In addition to trumpeter and arranger Terry, the band consisted at various times of Richard "Dick" Vance (trumpet), Edward "Eddie" Barefield (sax), James "Jimmy" Shirley (electric guitar), Elbert "Skippy" Williams (tenor sax) and Emmett Berry (trumpet), not to mention Doc Cheatham (trumpet) and Ben Thigpen (drums).

Raised in Cleveland, Vance (1914–1985) later worked with Fletcher Henderson, Chick Webb and Duke Ellington. Shirley (1913–1989), also from Cleveland, played with Clarence Profit, Ella Fitzgerald and Herman Chittison. Berry (1915–1993) moved to Cleveland as a child. Classically trained, he later joined Raymond Scott, Lionel Hampton and Count Basie. After attending high school in Cleveland, Williams (1916–1994) worked with Count Basie, Duke Ellington and Jimmy Mundy. Curiously, Barefield (1909–1991) came to Ohio from Iowa specifically to join the Virginia Ravens, an all-black territory band operated by an elderly white couple out of Genesee. He went on to work with Cab Calloway, Benny Carter and Duke Ellington.

Throughout the 1920s and 1930s, the name Austin Wylie (1893–1947) was synonymous with Cleveland's Golden Pheasant Restaurant, home base for his popular orchestra. Wylie seldom ventured out except for quick trips to New York City to record (sometimes with Piqua's Harry Reser on banjo). Several name musicians and bandleaders passed through the ranks of the Wylie band, including Claude Thornhill, Vaughn Monroe (1911–1973), Tony Pastor, Billy Butterfield* and Arthur Arshawsky (better known as Artie Shaw). At seventeen, Shaw took over as arranger and musical director for Wylie. When Shaw later formed his own group, Wylie managed him.

One of Wylie's major competitors was the Emerson Gill Orchestra, heard regularly on live remote radio broadcasts from Cleveland's Bamboo Gardens. When the Okeh label began making "location recordings" with mobile trucks in 1924, Gill's group was one of the first to sign up. Over the next two years, they recorded nine songs, including "Birmingham Bound" and "My Name Will Always Be Chickie" (with vocals by Pinkey Hunter).

The Marion Sears Orchestra was formed by saxophonist Marion Sears (1902–1989), brother of tenor sax titan "Big Al" Sears. (1910–1990). Both were born in Illinois, but in 1918 (when little Albert Omega was in second grade) the family moved to Zanesville. During the late 1920s, Al briefly worked in his big brother's band before playing with Chick Webb, Andy Kirk and Lionel Hampton. Meanwhile, Marion was hired as the house band at Cleveland Cedar Gardens (1924–1940s). His seven-piece ensemble quickly attracted some of the best up-and-coming musicians in the region.

In 1933, Springfield's Earle Warren*, just out of high school, was leading his own band in Columbus when he was recruited to join Marion Sears. Alto saxophonist Earl Bostic, having left his native Louisiana to join Clarence Olden's band in Columbus, also jumped to the Marion Sears Orchestra. Other musicians who filled out the roster were: trumpeter Freddie Webster, pianist and arranger Lavere "Buster" Harding, pianist Tadd Dameron* and saxophonist "Bull Moose" Jackson-. Harding (1912–1965) was a self-taught piano player from Canada who attended Cleveland Central High School. He later became an arranger for Teddy Wilson, Benny Goodman and Dizzy Gillespie.

A trumpet virtuoso in the Jimmie Lunceford Orchestra, Cleveland's Freddie Webster (1917–1947) died at thirty. More than forty years after his death, Dizzy Gillespie said Webster "probably had the best sound of the trumpet since the trumpet was invented, a sound that was alive, just alive and full of life!"

Drummer Bernard Joseph "Bernie" Cummins (1900–1986) got his start in his hometown of Akron and by 1919 was leading the Bernie Cummins Orchestra. His was one of the top dance bands during the next two decades. In addition to his brother, Walter (guitar/vocals), the group included future bandleaders Tommy Dorsey and Randy Brooks. The band's recorded output varies from the "hot" style of 1924 to the smooth sound of the 1930s.

While playing an engagement at the Stockton Club in Hamilton, Ohio,

during the summer of 1923, Cummins decided to take a job down the road at Cincinnati's Toadstool Inn. This prompted his lead trumpet player, George "Red" Bird, to quit the Cummins band and organize his own group to take over the Stockton Club engagement. Bird immediately headed to Chicago in search of the right musicians.

The Stockton Club was a notorious spot for bootleg booze, gambling and music. Supposedly operated by the Purple Gang, a particularly violent group of mobsters based in Detroit, it benefitted from its remote location (between Hamilton

Bandleader Bernie Cummins had a rule: no one in the band could date his vocalist, Jeanne Bennett. But that didn't stop his guitarist (and brother), Walter, from marrying her. *Jeanne Cummins.*

and Cincinnati) and its proximity to railroad and interurban lines. As a consequence, it became a gangland meeting place.

In addition to Bird, the band came to include Min Leibrook (tuba/bass) and Al Gandee (trombone). Leibrook, a Hamilton native, went on to play with the Paul Whiteman Orchestra; Gandee, from Cincinnati, later joined Dave Piet's Orchestra. A last-minute addition was a cornet player named Leon "Bix" Beiderbecke. They took their name, the Wolverines, from the Jelly Roll Morton song "Wolverine Blues."

When the club was shuttered temporarily as the result of a New Year's Eve free-for-all between rival gangsters, the Wolverines took a job playing at Doyle's Dance Academy in Cincinnati, where their "sock-time" rhythm quickly became a sensation among the young, working-class dancers. Then, on February 18, 1924, they made a quick trip to Gennett Studios in Richmond, Indiana, to record covers of some tunes popularized by the Original Dixieland Jazz Band. Beiderbecke was the star of these sessions, and soon everyone was talking about the "Young Man with a Horn."

An astute businessman, Cummins took over management of the Wolverines after a gig fell through, booking the band at colleges in Ohio and Indiana. In May, the band returned to Richmond to cut several more sides, including "Riverboat Shuffle," a tune it learned from composer Hoagy Carmichael, who just happened to be at the studio.

The Cincinnati-based Chubb-Steinberg Orchestra, led by violinist and vocalist Art Hicks, is best remembered for its fiery young cornetist, "Wild Bill" Davison. In March 1925, the band participated in a recording demonstration for radio listeners. While broadcasting live, it made a recording of "Because They All Love." The wax master was then played back for the audience. A record was subsequently pressed and issued by Gennett, with the notation on the label: "Played—Recorded—Broadcast at the Cincinnati Radio Show."

In actuality, the wax master would have been ruined during the playback process, so the version of the song that was released on record had actually been recorded at the Richmond studio in February. Nevertheless, through the medium of recording, and now radio, the market for jazz was expanding.

Radio and records were making overnight stars of dance bands from far-flung corners of the nation. Many restaurants, hotels and ballrooms originated remote radio broadcasts. However, the greatest exposure was given to those who were based in major cities. So Ohio musicians who wanted to make it big invariably had to leave home.

4
Jazz Goes to College

Wherever there was a heavy concentration of young adults, there was a demand for dance bands. Not surprisingly, colleges across the country became incubators for some of the best early jazz bands, rivaling those found in the big cities. That a disproportionate number of the great musicians were African American was due to this reality: music was one of the few areas in which they could succeed. As Fletcher Henderson, who had a college degree in chemistry, told his wife, "You better learn to play jazz or you won't make no money."

The "Great Migration" of southern blacks into the Northeast and Midwest fed the growth of African American communities and colleges in Ohio's major cities. The existence of such minority-owned or minority-friendly colleges as Wilberforce, Central State and Oberlin provided young African Americans with unparalleled educational opportunities.

Of course, not everyone was happy with the rise of jazz. When Miss Nelle I. Sharpe was appointed state supervisor of music in Ohio in 1922, her stated aim was to eliminate jazz. She predicted that it would triumph over "real music" unless she leveled the playing field. "Good music will win out over jazz if it has an equal chance," she declared, "but we cannot expect our pupils to discard jazz unless we give to the children who are going to be our future citizens a love for the good in music."[32]

Although born in Georgia, pianist, arranger and bandleader Horace W. Henderson (1904–1988), Fletcher's younger and, some say, more talented brother, first made his mark on the music world while attending Wilberforce College (now University). Located in Wilberforce, Ohio, it is the oldest private, historically black college in the nation, founded in 1856. As a result, it attracted the best African American educators, including W.E.B. Du Bois, and eager students from all over the country.

While a student at Wilberforce in the early 1920s, Horace (or "Little Smack," as he was dubbed; his brother was "Smack") formed a band called the Collegians, which eventually evolved into the Horace Henderson Orchestra. Among its members were such future jazz stars as Rex Stewart, Benny Carter, Ben Webster and, of course, Henderson himself.

Trumpeter Rex Stewart wasn't looking for an education when he came to Wilberforce; he was looking for his next gig. He later recalled that he was greeted by fellow New Yorker Freddie "Posey" Jenkins (1906–1978), fresh from the Jenkins

Horace Henderson's Wilberforce Collegians weren't the only game in town, as this early poster shows. *DS.*

Orphanage Band. Jenkins first played trumpet with Edgar Hayes (1904–1979) for less than a year before jumping to Henderson's ensemble in 1924. He remained with the Collegians until he joined Duke Ellington in 1928.

Hayes, a pianist and arranger, had a band called the Blue Grass Buddies, which essentially paved the way for Henderson's band. At one time, it included clarinetist Garvin Bushell·.

Others in the lineup with Stewart were Shelton Hemphill (trumpet), William "Bill" Beason (drums) and Jimmy King (drums). Hemphill had toured with Bessie Smith and would go on to work with Chick Webb, Louis Armstrong and Duke Ellington. Beason came to the band in 1924 and later played with "Jelly Roll" Morton and Don Redman and replaced the terminally ill Chick Webb in Ella Fitzgerald's band. Little-known King, according to Joe Jones (no slouch himself), was the most musical drummer he ever heard but died in his twenties.

Benny Carter had already worked with famed pianists Willie "the Lion" Smith and Earl Hines when he joined Henderson's Collegians in 1924. He could play alto sax, trumpet and clarinet with the best of them and was also a talented composer, arranger and bandleader. He never actually enrolled at Wilberforce, though, and left the band after two years. During Carter's tenure, "a little fella" named Ben Webster became the band's "valet." He would later gain fame as an exceptional tenor saxophonist with Duke Ellington.

By the time Henderson quit to join the Sammy Stewart Orchestra, the band was known as the Dixie Stompers. In 1928, Henderson reorganized the Collegians with Youngstown's Myron "Tiny" Bradshaw ♪ as the vocalist. However, Henderson soon had left it behind once again to work with his older brother, Fletcher, as an arranger.

Drummer George Russell (1923–2009) was invited to audition for the Collegians but failed, possibly because his drum kit was substandard. Given a second chance, he won a position in the band. "Back then the black universities scouted for jazz musicians just as they scout for athletes now," Russell recalled. However, since he was only sixteen, he was enrolled in the college's high school (as was Garvin Bushell) and commuted daily from his home in Cincinnati, sixty miles away! Russell went on to be a highly regarded jazz pianist and composer.

Ernie Wilkins, John "Willie" Cook and Eli "Lucky" Thompson were also members of the Collegians during 1938–41, when Russell was the drummer. A pianist and violinist before turning to the sax, Wilkins, from St. Louis, developed into one of the top bop tenor players and a composer/arranger for everyone from Harry James to Count Basie. Tenor sax man Thompson, down from Detroit, bridged the era between swing and bebop, playing with Lionel Hampton, Lucky Millinder and Count Basie. Cook had grown up in East Chicago, Illinois. He went on to play lead trumpet with the likes of Duke Ellington, Dizzy Gillespie and Count Basie before making his home in Sweden.

When Frank Foster ♪ was ready to go to college in 1946, minorities were not admitted to the Cincinnati College-Conservatory (and he was late applying to Oberlin) so he wound up at Wilberforce and joined the Collegians. By that time, Jimmy Wilkins, Ernie's brother, was leading the eighteen-piece band. Foster quickly began contributing arrangements and playing sax. Trumpeter/pianist Charles Freeman Lee (1927–   ) out of New York was also in the Collegians during Foster's tenure, and they became good friends. Lee later played with Foster, Snooky Young, Sonny Stitt, Eddie "Lockjaw" Davis and James Moody.

Eugene Edward "Snooky" Young⁻ was rated by trumpeter Thad Jones, who should know, as "the number one man" when it came to playing first trumpet. Born in Dayton, he started out with his family band, the Young Snappy Six. Although he never attended Wilberforce, he played with the Collegians before moving on to the bands of Chick Carter, Jimmie Lunceford, Lionel Hampton and Count Basie. In his later years, Young continued to play despite becoming profoundly deaf.

A number of other notable musicians came out of Wilberforce College at different times. Singer James Andrew "Jimmy" Rushing (1901–1972), perhaps the first blues singer to ever enter college, became the featured vocalist with the Count Basie Orchestra.

A musically ambitious student, Mississippi-born William Grant Still (1895–1978) enrolled at Wilberforce following graduation from high school at age sixteen. He was not happy there (he wanted to go to Oberlin), but his mother insisted. Nevertheless, he did acquire a practical education in music, although he bristled at the many restrictions the church-owned institution imposed on student behavior. After leaving Wilberforce, he was hired by booking agent Tom Howard on the strength of his abilities on the oboe and cello. He soon was to become the "Dean of African American Composers."

Meanwhile, sixty miles away in Columbus, another band called the Collegians formed at the Ohio State University in the early 1920s. Led by pianist and vocalist Robert "Bob" Royce (1902–1973), it became the Royce-Taylor Orchestra with the addition of vocalist and sax player Thal Taylor from Illinois. Unlike the Wilberforce group, this was a white dance band. It also included some notable players, including Carl Agee (trumpet), Joe "Country" Washburn (vocals/bass/tuba), Arthur Wilson "Dusty" Rhodes (drums/vocals), Guy "Hogey" Workman (trombone/vocals), Thomas Parker Gibbs (vocals/clarinet/tenor sax) and Ernest "Red" Ingle (vocals/ violin/sax/ clarinet). They, too, came from all over the country—and not necessarily to attend college.

Scott Gibbs, son of Parker, noted that after the band had been in existence for several years, "virtually all of the Ted Weems Orchestra were recruited from Ohio State University, where the Weems band was playing when Weems came to town and had a revolt of his band members who wanted more money…Ted Weems picked up almost all of that band to go on the road with him (they were thrilled to work for a big time band, even for the lousy wages Ted was paying)."[33]

Washburn grew up in Texas. After joining the Ted Weems, he became a songwriter as well, with "One Dozen Roses," "I Saw Essau" and "We'll Sing the Old Songs" to his credit. Ernest Jansen "Red" Ingle (1906–1965), from Toledo, started on the violin at age five and received occasional tutoring from family friend Fritz Kreisler. Before joining Royce, he toured with Jean Goldkette. Perry Como, Weems's featured vocalist, called Ingle "one of the most talented men I've ever met."

"Dusty" Rhodes (or Roads/Rhoades) has been described as a "spirited" vocalist. When Royce's band played at Valley Dale Ballroom in Columbus, Dusty was a crowd favorite, leading them in college fight songs. After a few years with Weems, he was hired by Charlie Agnew and his NBC Orchestra. Until Perry Como joined, Parker Gibbs was the best singer in the Weems organization. In 1929, Gibbs had a million-selling hit record of "Piccolo Pete."

Thal Taylor left Weems to join Art Kassel and his "Kassels in the Air" Orchestra as a featured vocalist. However, his partner, Bob Royce, eventually returned to Columbus and became a celebrated architect, designing many homes in the suburb of Upper Arlington.

While at Ohio State, "Hogey" Workman was a member of the highly regarded Scarlet Mask Orchestra. Founded as early as 1920 to accompany musical comedies staged by the Scarlet Mask Club, it ranged from fourteen to twenty pieces. Eventually, the musicians broke away and became an independent ensemble. In 1928–29, the Scarlet Mask Orchestra performed on the SS *Calgarie* for a cruise of Scandinavia, Germany and England and the SS *Leviathan* for two ocean crossings.

Of the bands active at Ohio State during this period, only one, Harold Ortli & His Ohio State Collegians, made it into the recording studio. In 1925, Cleveland-born Ortli heard about the Okeh Records auditions when he was at home on a break from school. He quickly summoned the rest of his band to Lake Erie for a session in which they cut two very hot tunes: "My Daddy Rocks Me (With One Steady Roll)" and "I Couldn't Get to It in Time." The former was originally recorded by African American blues singer Trixie Smith in 1922.

Although colleges across the nation were turning out hundreds of jazz bands and thousands of jazz musicians—from the Prairie View Co-Eds to Les Brown's Duke Blue Devils—it would be several decades before the practice became anything more than extracurricular.

5
The Rise of Swing

The 1920s had been the jazz age. Young people danced to celebrate their own liberation and the country's prosperity. During the Great Depression of the 1930s, however, they danced as an escape from the austerity and bleakness of the times. Movies and dancing were cheap forms of entertainment. Meanwhile, the music continued to evolve.

When swing was introduced in 1935, some existing bands changed with the times or simply retired. During the late 1920s, more space was given to improvised solos (riffing), although this style was less popular among dancers. The development of call-and-response patterns—originally found in African folk music—enabled the big bands to create more excitement, as one section of the band would play a two- or four-bar phrase that would be answered by another section. There was a range of styles among swing bands, with some dominated by strong instrumentalists and others by star vocalists.

When Sidney Bechet entered Okeh Studios on July 30, 1923, history was made. For the first time on record, a musician stepped out of his ensemble role to play an extended solo. On "Wild Cat Blues" and "Kansas City Man Blues," Bechet's soprano sax soars over the accompanying orchestra as he exhibits his amazing gift for improvisation.

Up until then, the model for jazz groups had been the New Orleans–style ensemble. Essentially, everyone improvised together. Although an individual musician might take a short break, no one dominated the piece. For example, in Joe "King" Oliver's band, Oliver (on first cornet) would start a line and let Louis Armstrong (on second cornet) complete it. But it wouldn't be long before others were stepping out as well, especially Armstrong. It was another milestone. However, this new form would be known as "Chicago style."

But the musicians didn't forget the dancers. As an old Polish proverb says, "The man who can't dance thinks the band is no good." While dancing wasn't a uniquely midwestern form of entertainment, it was probably embraced with more enthusiasm there than anywhere else in the country. In 1932, eighteen-year-old Marie Behm, from the farming community of New Bremen, attended as many as four dances a week. Among the dance halls she regularly mentioned in her diary were the Pier at Gordon State Park, Lock II Dance Hall, National Guard Armory, Eagle Park Pavilion, Kuenning's Grove and Knights of Pythias Hall—all within eight miles of her home.

Since Ohio was a good market for bands, it should not be surprising that so many successful bandleaders came from the Buckeye State. A native of Canton, Enoch Light (1905–1978) attended Johns Hopkins University before starting his own band in the 1920s. For the most part, he catered to the hotel trade, although he briefly led a swing band during the 1940s. Later Light was A&R chief and vice-president of Grand Award Records before founding Command Records in 1959, purveyors of "ping-pong" stereo. After selling the Command label in 1965, Light formed a new label, Project 3, and recorded a series of note-by-note re-creations of hits from the big band era.

Although born in Kentucky, Clyde McCoy (1903–1990) grew up just across the river in Portsmouth. Starting on the trombone, he switched to trumpet at age ten and within a few years was working in theaters and on riverboats. McCoy began employing a mute around 1922 and soon become known for his "wah-wah" sound (which inspired the later wah-wah pedal for electric guitars). Forming his own orchestra, McCoy had an enormous hit in 1931 with his recording of "Sugar Blues." It sold more than one million copies and became his signature tune. McCoy performed it on miniature trumpet.[34]

Originally from Coalton, Isham Jones* was an accomplished bandleader and sax player but an even more successful composer, with more than one hundred songs to his credit. In 1924 alone, he wrote "I'll See You in My Dreams," "It Had to Be You," "The One I Love Belongs to Somebody Else" and "Spain" (the last three in a single night!). The Jones organization was one of the first bands signed by the Music Corporation of America, enabling him to obtain bookings throughout the country. Soon, he was also touring England, where he was already well known for his recordings. Some of these were considered musically daring, especially his collaborations with the Three X Sisters.

The Clicquot Club Eskimos were led by Piqua-native Harry F. Reser (1896–1965), possibly the best banjo player of the jazz age. A long-running hit on NBC radio in New York City (1925–35), the show was sponsored by Clicquot (pronounced "klee-ko"), a beverage manufacturer. Reser, a top session player, simultaneously led other bands, such as Harry Reser and His Six Jumping Jacks, which inspired the Hoosier Hotshots, Spike Jones and His City Slickers, Freddie "Schnickelfritz" Fisher and similar novelty groups.

Drummer Barney Rappaport (1900–1970) shortened his name to Barney Rapp and organized his first band in New England in the 1920s, before relocating to Cincinnati. When his vocalist (and wife) Ruby Wright became pregnant, he replaced her with a local girl, Doris Kappelhoff, whom he (or maybe bandleader Les Brown) renamed Doris Day after hearing her sing the song "Day by Day." He also gave the Clooney Sisters (Rosemary and Betty) their first break and recommended them to Tony Pastor. With his own nightclub, the Sign of the Drum, as a home base, Rapp was frequently heard over WLW Radio.

Bandleader and saxophonist Frederick "Freddy" Martin (1906–1983) spent his childhood moving in and out of a Springfield orphanage. He planned to study journalism at Ohio State but got sidetracked when Guy Lombardo heard his band and recommended it for jobs he could not fill. Martin popularized a style of sweet music that was called "tenor bands" because of his use of an all-tenor sax section. However, his real success resulted from a recording of Tchaikovsky's B-flat piano concerto (with lyrics added), released as "Tonight We Love" (1941).

Blue Barron (1913–2005) was born Harry Freidman in Cleveland. He attended Ohio University (where he met Sammy Kaye) and eventually decided to carve out a career in the music business. Following graduation, he returned to Cleveland to become a booking agent, specializing in "sweet" (sometimes called "Mickey Mouse") bands such as Guy Lombardo's, Kay Kyser's and Kaye's (the last of which he also managed). His tagline was "Music of Yesterday and Today, Styled the Blue Barron Way."

Alvin McBurney (1908–2004), stage name Alvino Rey, is sometimes credited with being the father of the pedal steel guitar (and in 1932, he played the first electrified guitar ever heard on a coast-to-coast broadcast). He did not use it for country music but rather big band, swing music and even jazz. Born in California, he moved to Cleveland as a child. After high school, he headed for New York City. Soon, he was playing electric guitar in various name orchestras, including those of Horace Heidt, Russ Morgan and Freddy Martin. Forming his own group with the King Sisters, he made a name for himself in Los Angeles and on an ABC TV series.

Originally from Akron, Vaughn Monroe (1911–1973) was a successful singer, bandleader, actor and radio and TV star. Among his hit recordings were his signature tune, "Racing with the Moon" (1941), as well as "In the Still of the Night" (1939), "There I Go" (1941), "There I've Said It Again" (1945), "Let It Snow, Let It Snow, Let It Snow" (1946), "Riders in the Sky" (1949), "Someday (You'll Want Me to Want You)" (1949) and "In the Middle of the House" (1956). In 1944 alone, Monroe sold over five million records.

When the Dorsey brothers had their famous falling out, Jimmy needed somebody to take over Tommy's trombone chair in the band. After auditioning dozens of other musicians, they settled on a sixteen-year-old kid who had sat in with them one night: Bobby Byrne (1918–2006). Byrne was born in Pleasant Corners, just outside Columbus, to a renowned music teacher, Clarence Byrn. His father drilled perfection into him, and it was a trait that carried over into his professional life. The tension this created within his band may have undermined his ultimate success as a bandleader. However, as a musician and arranger, he was one of the best.

In historian George Simon's opinion, "Only God can make a tree and only men can play good jazz."[35] He was wrong, of course. Given the opportunity, women can play anything. But, historically, they have not always had the same doors open to them. (It wasn't until 1973 that a woman was allowed to join the Ohio State University Marching Band!) However, that did not stop a number of pioneering female musicians from knocking on those doors, anyway—and sometimes kicking them open.[36]

Although not the first, The Ingénues was a groundbreaking, fifteen- to nineteen-piece all-girl orchestra from Youngstown (home of an earlier group, Barry's Novelty Girls). Organized in 1925 by vaudeville producer E.G. Sherman, it initially played throughout the Midwest and eventually toured Europe, South Africa, Asia and Australia. Two years later, The Ingénues was headlining the Ziegfeld Follies, where for one number the band performed on twelve white baby grand pianos. Known for its members' beauty ("the Band Beautiful") and versatility (they all doubled on brass, strings and woodwinds), the Ingénues included jazz, Dixieland, Tin Pan Alley and light classical pieces in its repertoire.

The star soloist of the Ingénues was "trick trombonist" Paula Jones (who also played banjo and accordion). During the 1930s, trumpeter Louise Sorenson was praised in *DownBeat*, which noted that she "can play every instrument in the band and has exceptional knowledge of harmony and how to handle orchestrating for a band with so much versatility."[37] Sometimes billed as the "Female Paul Whitemans of Syncopation," the women were also expected to sing, dance and dress spectacularly. However, all-female groups were seldom regarded as more than a novelty act, despite the high caliber of their musicianship.

Ohio contributed members to other all-girl bands, as well. Frances Klein Siskin (1915–   ) of Cleveland played trumpet with Ina Rae Hutton's All-Girl Traveling Band. Multi-instrumentalist Fern Spaulding Jaros (1908–2010), born in Loveland, toured with Ina Rae Hutton, Babe Egan and Ada Leonard and Her All-Girl Orchestra. She also performed with the Chicago Symphony.

Columbus-based Rose Thall and Her Radio Girls' Orchestra was formed in 1930 by pianist Rose Thall (1907–2004) and drummer Mac McArthur, both of whom had previously been members of Babe Egan's Hollywood Redheads on the West Coast. Billed as the "Sunshine Girl," Thall also served as staff pianist for WCAH radio. Bexley's Rose Blane (1911–1974), née Blank, sang with an all-girl band before joining Arthur Lyman's Orchestra and settling in California as Lyman's wife.

Russian immigrant Phil Spitalny (1890–1970), who came to Cleveland with his family, was the man behind the most commercially successful (and "least jazzy," to quote Sherrie Tucker)[38] all-girl orchestra. Founded in 1934, Spitalny's group also included many first-rate musicians. Flutist Frances Blaisdell, for one, was the first female wind player admitted to the Juilliard School of Music and the first to perform as a soloist with the New York Philharmonic. However, the emphasis was on femininity and sweetness, as evidenced by the name of their radio program, *The Hour of Charm.*

While they occasionally performed such jazz standards as "Tiger Rag," Spitalny's emphasis was on wholesomeness. In fact, the women had to sign contracts promising not to marry for two years (vocalist Maxine Marlowe, "discovered" at Ohio State, actually drafted the "vow"). The mother of Sylvania native Chip Davis, creator of Manheim Steamroller, was once a trombonist with Spitalny's group.

However, the most "famous" Buckeye to get her start in an all-girl band was Steubenville's Dorothy Sloop Heflick (1913–1998). A talented pianist and occasional singer, "Sloopy," as she was known professionally, went on the road with the Southland Rhythm Girls after high school and ended up in New Orleans. She found work at Dixie's Bar of Music on Bourbon Street, backing singer and clarinet player Yvonne "Dixie" Fasnacht. Among her fans was songwriter Bert Russell Berns. One evening while Heflick was playing, Berns heard a customer shout out, "Hang on, Sloopy!" He soon incorporated the line into a song, "My Girl Sloopy," which became a number one hit as "Hang on Sloopy" for the Dayton-based rock band The McCoys in 1965.

It was lyricist Lee Adams, a Mansfield-born graduate of the Ohio State University, who posed the musical question, "Why can't they dance like we

Dorothy "Dottie" Sloop, the woman who inspired the song "Hang on Sloopy," accompanies singer Dixie Fasnacht at her Bar of Music in New Orleans, circa 1957. *Brett Ruland.*

did? What's wrong with Sammy Kaye?" And it was Mount Vernon's Paul Lynde (as befuddled Harry MacAfee) who sang it in the 1960 Broadway show *Bye Bye, Birdie.* The question was rhetorical, of course, but every jazz lover (and, presumably, many theatergoers) knew the answer. By that time, Sammy Kaye' was considered strictly squaresville. However, it was also a compliment to Kaye's enormous success.

Kaye was the bestselling bandleader in the country from 1946 to 1955, when big bands were on their way out. His band, originally formed while he was a student at Ohio University, was built around his "sweet" sound, with an emphasis on singers and vocal group numbers. Between 1937 and 1971, Kaye recorded more than 1,300 songs on a variety of labels. In 1941 alone, he scored two majors hits with "Daddy" and "Dream Valley." Supposedly, Kaye was such a tyrant that his entire band once quit on him, but he knew what the public wanted.

6

Singing Jazz

In 1942, the American Federation of Musicians imposed a ban on all recording. Combined with wartime travel restrictions, most bands were hard-pressed to keep their music before the general public. However, the ban did not stop all recording. Singers, not being members of the union, could continue to cut records backed by vocal groups that sang the instrumental parts of a song. Although the results weren't always satisfying, it did boost the popularity of such vocalists as Dick Haymes and Frank Sinatra.

"The term 'Jazz singer' is a dubious one," according to critic Gene Lees.

> *If it means anything specific, it surely denotes someone who can improvise with the voice. In a well-made song, the intervals of the music bear a significant relationship to the natural inflections of the words, and to alter the melody compromises the meaning and diminishes the dramatic effect of the song as a whole. Unfortunately, that is exactly what all too many "Jazz singers" do.*

Crowther and Pinfold contend that "without Louis Armstrong and without his cross-over to popular song, jazz might have ended as a mere footnote to the 1920s."[39] By 1929, his singing was featured as much as his trumpet playing (which encouraged a whole host of other trumpeters to sing). More than anyone else, Armstrong was responsible for trailblazing the role of the jazz vocalist.

All of the great jazz singers (Crosby, Sinatra, Fitzgerald) readily acknowledge their debt to Satchmo. But Armstrong admitted he also learned from Crosby. And Crosby said he also learned from "Skin" Young. What was that? Skin who?

Well, in 1926, Bing Crosby and Al Rinker (brother of jazz singer Mildred Bailey) had dropped out of college to work as a vocal duo. While appearing in a Los Angeles vaudeville house, several members of Paul Whiteman's Orchestra saw them and recommended the singers to their boss. According to Crosby, he had been to see Whiteman several times and was blown away by the "sensational singing style" of Austin "Skin" Young (1898–1936) of Columbus. When Whiteman offered him a job, he jumped at the opportunity to study his idol up close. Young can be heard on many of Whiteman's recordings, including "Felix the Cat" and "Chloe" (both 1928).

Of course, Armstrong's gritty vocals owed a debt to the many African American blues singers who had preceded him. As it so happened, the "first" (all such claims are tentative) person to make a vocal blues recording was Mamie Smith° of Cincinnati. Born Mamie Robinson, she had already left home to tour with the Four Dancing Mitchells, a white vaudeville act, at the age of ten. By the time she was twenty, she had married a waiter named William "Smitty" Smith and was singing in Harlem clubs. She was thirty-seven when she first entered a New York studio and recorded "Crazy Blues" for Okeh Records in 1920. In less than a year, it sold one million copies.

CRAZY BLUES

By PERRY BRADFORD

MAMIE SMITH AND HER JAZZ HOUNDS

Get this number for your phonograph on Okeh Record No. 4169

Mamie Smith & Her Jazz Hounds took the country by storm with the 1920 recording "Crazy Blues," opening the door for other blues singers. *DS.*

Mamie Smith & Her Jazz Hounds, the "Queen of the Blues," toured the United States and Europe. In 1929, she made an appearance in an early sound film, *Jail House Blues*. However, in 1931, Smith retired at age forty-eight. Eight years later, she began a brief career in movies, starting with *Paradise in Harlem* in 1939 and ending with *Because I Love You* in 1943. She passed away in New York three years afterward.

One direct beneficiary of Smith's success was "the Original" Bessie Brown (1890–1955). Born in Cleveland, she was a blues, jazz and cabaret singer who has been compared to Sophie Tucker. On her recordings, she was accompanied by such stars as Coleman Hawkins, Fletcher Henderson, Rex Stewart, Buster Bailey and Clarence Williams. Brown's best-known song was "There Ain't Much Good in the Best of Men Nowdays" (1926).

A quartet of Ohio singers also turned heads with their fresh and radical approach to singing: the Mills Brothers[*]. One of the greatest vocal groups of all time, their influence on both jazz and pop singing is incalculable. "They just turned everything upside down," according to James Maher.[40] Tony Bennett recalled that when he was growing up in Queens, New York, he would often hear Irish families imitating the Mills Brothers. Both Frank Sinatra's and Dean Martin's earliest recordings are clear imitations of Harry Mills. And Harry, of course, was imitating Louis Armstrong.

The story of the Mills Brothers began in Piqua, during the early years of the twentieth century. Four brothers were born to John and Eathel Mills. John Sr. owned a barbershop and, more importantly, led his own barbershop quartet, the Four Kings of Harmony. Naturally, the boys grew up singing, with Harry adding little flourishes on the kazoo. However, during an amateur contest at the local Mays Opera House, he suddenly realized he didn't have it with him, so he cupped his hands around his mouth and imitated a trumpet.

That's the legend, anyway. This spontaneous act was an immediate hit with the audience, so all of his brothers also began to imitate instruments: John Jr., who sang bass, would imitate the tuba; baritone Harry stuck with the trumpet; Herbert was the second trumpet; and Donald was the trombone. John Jr. also accompanied them on the ukulele and, later, the guitar. The Mills Brothers become well known not only for their ability to imitate instruments but also for their close four-part harmonies and their scat singing. They sang wherever they could: nightclubs, theaters, tent shows, dance halls—even on a platform erected outside a roadhouse in Columbus.

Then, in 1928, they accompanied the local Harold Greenamyer Orchestra on a trip to Cincinnati to audition for radio station WLW. Greenamyer was told thanks but no thanks. However, the Mills Brothers were hired, quickly becoming local radio stars. When Duke Ellington heard them while playing a job in Cincinnati, he arranged for them to be signed to Okeh Records. An audition for William S. Paley at CBS Radio in New York resulted in a three-year contract. The Mills Brothers became the first African American performers to have a network radio show.

Their very first recording on Brunswick Records, a cover of the Original Dixieland Jass Band's "Tiger Rag," was a nationwide hit, shooting to number one on the charts. Many others followed. On records and radio, it was also explained to the listeners that the only actual instrument was the guitar; the trumpet, sax and string bass were products of the brothers' voices.

The Mills Brothers recorded "I'll Be Around" in 1943, but no one paid much attention to the flipside, a number that they had recorded in fifteen minutes, until a disc jockey played it on a whim. "Paper Doll," written by Hamilton, Ohio songwriter Johnny S. Black in 1915 but not published until 1930, became their biggest hit ever, selling an astounding six million copies.[11]

Una Mae Carlisle was considered an exceptionally gifted musician, and in 1932 she was heard by "Fats" Waller, who put her on his WLW radio show, *Fat's Rhythm Club*. He also used her in his club dates. In 1939, Carlisle recorded "I Can't Give You Anything but Love" with Waller. Later that same year, she traveled to Europe with the Blackbirds Revue, where she recorded for Leonard Feather and did film work in France. While there, she had her own nightclub in Montmartre and studied harmony at the Sorbonne.

One of the most influential of all Ohio jazz singers was Jon Hendricks. Born in Newark and reared in Toledo, he sometimes sang accompanied by family friend Art Tatum. After World War II, Hendricks went to New York to become a singer and composer, taking Charlie Parker up on his invitation to look him up. In 1957, he formed the legendary vocal trio Lambert, Hendricks & Ross with Dave Lambert and Annie Ross. Although they broke up after six years, they remain the model for all jazz vocal groups.

Hendricks may not have invented vocalese, but he is the acknowledged master. Rather than merely faking the sound of musical instruments à la the Mills Brothers or scatting with nonsense words, vocalese adds lyrics to replace the notes in jazz instrumentals—one syllable per note. And no one has done it better than Hendricks. Al Jarreau has hailed him as "pound-for-pound the best jazz singer on the planet—maybe that's ever been."

For the most part, however, vocalese is used to replicate famous jazz solos that were originally created by others. Richard Sudhalter discovered vocalese versions of Bix Beiderbecke's solo on "Singin' the Blues," dating back to 1934. It remained something of a novelty until Eddie Jefferson allegedly turned James Moody's alto sax solo on "I'm in the Mood for Love" into a vocalese solo, "Moody's Mood for Love." Vocalist King Pleasure (1922–1981) made it into a classic recording in 1952 and inspired Hendricks to change his own approach to songwriting.

Born Clarence Beeks in Tennessee, Pleasure was a mysterious man (Will Friedwald called him "a wack job") who grew up in Cincinnati and first came to notice when he set words to Lester Young's "DB Blues." He also scored a hit with his own lyrics to Charlie "Bird" Parker's composition "Parker's Mood" (1953), in which he predicted Parker's death. Pleasure did little to advance his own career, seldom recording or performing in public. However, he did manage to record a few songs with Hendricks and Ross before his premature "retirement" in 1962.

Because singers are tied to (you might say "burdened with") the lyric, they have less freedom than other jazz musicians—except when they "scat" (i.e. dispense with the words and sing improvised sounds). Consequently, there have been few "true" jazz vocalists. Most are pop and blues singers, often exceptional balladeers, who introduce jazz elements into their vocalizing when they can. But true improvisation is held to a minimum. As with vocalese, scatting is not a style that all jazz singers embrace. Mark Murphy has said, "People are used to songs being an unchanging line of storytelling…Scatting or improvising…It makes an audience work harder."

Perhaps one of the most famous scat singers, though hardly the first, was Benjamin Sherman "Scatman" Crothers (1910–1986), originally from Indiana.[12] Crothers got his nickname while performing on his own daily fifteen-minute radio broadcast on WFMK in Dayton. When asked what he wanted to call the program, he replied, "Call Me Scat Man." A feature of each show was when Crothers replaced the lyrics with improvised "shabadebedebedo" or "dobedebedebam."

In an attempt to overcome the limits of vocalese and scat, avant-garde vocalist Jay Clayton (1941–   ), born Judith Colantone in Youngstown, turned to "free jazz" for inspiration. After studying at Miami University, she and her husband, percussionist Frank Clayton, began presenting Jazz at the Loft in their New York City apartment in 1967. She quickly acquired a reputation for her use of her own personal (wordless) singing style.

Born James Victor Scott in Cleveland, Little Jimmy Scott was late receiving the recognition he deserves. Despite being an amazing vocalist (Madonna called him the only singer who could make her cry), Scott had difficulty finding the right venue for his talent. He also had more than his share of problems with recording companies when Savoy Records released and then abruptly recalled his albums *Falling in Love Is Beautiful* (1962) and *The Source* (1969).

Among Scott's many admirers have been Billie Holiday, Dinah Washington and Ohio's own Nancy Wilson*. In fact, she has long maintained that "there would be no Nancy Wilson if it weren't for Little Jimmy Scott." Born in Chillicothe, Wilson grew up in Columbus. Her debut single, "Guess Who I Saw Today" (1960), was such a success that she released five albums in the span of two years. It is the diversity of her recorded output that makes it difficult to classify Wilson. To some, she is a jazz singer, to others a pop singer and to still others a blues singer. However, she has always seen herself as a song stylist who acted out her songs.

A jazz, blues, gospel and soul singer from Springfield, Ada Lee is better known in Canada, where she has lived since the early 1960s. While studying voice at the Dayton Conservatory of Music, she sang with the Bus Palmer Band on weekends. Following graduation from Wilberforce University, Lee worked some local dates with both Count Basie and Lionel Hampton. In 1960, George Wein, producer of the Newport Jazz Festival, became her manager. A year later, she released her debut album on Atlantic Records to a four-star review from *Billboard Magazine*.

Lima-born Helen O'Connell (1920–1993) left Ohio with the Jimmy Richard's band and was given a regular radio show in St. Louis. From there,

A very young Nancy Wilson performs with vibraphonist Sylvester Burch and, possibly, drummer Taylor Orr. *LFTJ*.

she went to New York City, where she was discovered by Jimmy Dorsey in 1938. Almost immediately, O'Connell had a hit with "All of Me." However, her popularity really took off when Dorsey teamed her with Bob Eberly for a series of duets. Among their best-remembered songs were "Amapola" (1941), "Yours" (1941), "Green Eyes" (1941) and "Tangerine" (1942). In 1940 and 1941, O'Connell was voted best female singer by the readers of *DownBeat*. The only real complaint against her was that she took the spotlight off Dorsey.

Marion Mann (1914–2004) was born in Columbus and was singing with a female trio on local radio when she was recruited for Cleveland's Emerson Gill Orchestra. While with Gill, Bob Crosby (Bing's brother) invited her to join his group, the Bobcats. From 1938 to 1940, Mann recorded at least thirty-five songs with this band, including "The Big Base Viol" (1938), "At a Little Hot Dog Stand" (1939) and "With the Wind and the Rain in Your Hair" (1940). After she was seriously injured in an automobile accident, she stopped touring and joined the cast of the Chicago radio program *Don McNeil's Breakfast Club*.

The last vocalist to tour and record with Jimmy Dorsey, Claire "Shanty" Hogan (1927–2000) later took a job as composer "Cy" Coleman's "girl Friday." He, in turn, produced two remarkable albums for her, *Just Imagine* (1956) and *Boozers and Losers* (1967). The latter is considered her masterpiece and displays

Vocalist Marion Mann performs with Bob Crosby and the Bobcats. *LFTJ.*

Boozers and Losers vocalist Claire Hogan with her then-husband, saxophonist Johnny Bothwell, in New York City, 1946. *WG-LOC.*

her considerable skills as a blues, torch and, sometimes, jazz singer. Born in Canton, Hogan's career began when she beat out five hundred other vocalists for a job in the Boyd Raeburn Band. Then, in 1949, she joined Jimmy Dorsey, with whom she recorded a dozen or so songs. She also performed briefly with Count Basie and Gene Krupa before giving up show business.

Although she was always a Kentucky girl at heart, things didn't start happening for singer Rosemary Clooney (1928–2002) until she moved to Cincinnati with her family when she was thirteen. In 1945, she and her sister, Betty, began performing on WLW radio. Six years later, she finally scored a hit with "Come On-A My House" (1951), a song she despised. Clooney soon became a movie and TV star, while continuing her recording career off and on until the end of her life. Her reputation as a jazz singer primarily stems from her 1956 collaboration with Duke Ellington and Billy Strayhorn, *Blue Rose*, and her comeback in the late 1970s.

According to record producer Joel Dorn, Austin Cromer (1930–1999) is known as "the guy who sang 'Over the Rainbow' with Dizzy's band." Dizzy, of course, was trumpeter Dizzy Gillespie. "But just when fame and success were staring him in the face," Dorn wrote, "fate conjured up a series of events that forced Austin to abandon singing." Actually, Cromer was from

Detroit originally and had been a member of the legendary vocal group the Ravens during the 1950s. But when he was rediscovered by Atlantic Records in 1965, he was working on a construction gang in Columbus and taking gigs where he could find them. The resulting album only hints at how great he was; the live recordings of Gillespie's big band during their South American tour are the ones to watch for.

Song stylist Betty St. Claire (1927–1972) was born Betty Waddell in Columbus. As a teenager, she won the "Miss Bronzeville" beauty pageant. She also sang with visiting bands while attending East High School. Following graduation, she was taken to New York City by local promoter William "Bubbles" Holloway. En route, he renamed her "St. Clair," after St. Clair Avenue, where she grew up. Soon, St. Claire was singing with Noble Sissle's USO troupe,[43] pianist Errol Garner (to whom she was briefly married) and Dizzy Gillespie, before settling into New York nightclubs. She released four very good albums before dropping out of the music scene.

Albert Alan "Al" Smith (1936–   ) holds the distinction of being the first person to release an album on the Bluesville label, *Hear My Blues* (1959). Born in Columbus, he was orphaned as a youth and lived in New Orleans from ages ten to seventeen. As a foster child, he moved frequently and never put down any roots. Working his way to Newark, New Jersey, he caught the attention of Eddie "Lockjaw" Davis at a jam session. Although Smith considered himself a gospel singer, Davis hustled him into the studio to record his magnificent debut album. A year later, the label released a follow-up, *Midnight Special*, and then Smith vanished, lost in a sea of other Al Smiths.

For many, the highlight of the 1992 movie *White Men Can't Jump* is the trio singing the gospel tune "Just a Closer Walk with Thee" a cappella under the credits. The Venice Beach Boys, as they are billed, were composed of Sonny Craver from Columbus, Jon Hendricks from Newark/Toledo and Bill Henderson from Chicago. Craver remained in his hometown long enough to kick off a career as a singer and start his own record label, Stanson. Starting at seventeen, Craver toured with Stomp Gordon, King Kollax and the Harmonaires. Later, he replaced Joe Williams in Count Basie's Orchestra.

Doris Mary Ann von Kappelhoff (1924–   ) from Cincinnati, later Doris Day, was pursuing a career as a dancer until a 1937 traffic accident damaged her legs. While recovering from her injuries, she began taking voice lessons. Soon, she was touring with Les Brown and His Band of Renown. Although she was only fifteen, she had convinced the bandleader she was eighteen. While Day's work in Hollywood, which included several pop hits, most notably "Que Sera Sera (Whatever Will Be, Will Be)" (1956), tends to overshadow

A twenty-two-year-old Doris Day with bandleader Les Brown at New York City's Aquarium Jazz Club, 1946. *WG-LOC.*

her earlier accomplishments, she was actually a credible jazz singer. Witness her radio transcriptions made with the Page Cavanaugh Trio in 1948.

Born Theresa Breuer (1931–2007) in Toledo, Teresa Brewer (her professional name) was one of the most popular singers of the 1950s, with more than six hundred recordings to her credit. Her 1949 recording, "Music! Music! Music!" with the Dixieland All-Stars, was just the first of a string of pop hits that typecast her as a singer of perky songs. However, in the 1980s, she reinvented herself as a jazz vocalist on a series of albums released on the Amsterdam label, owned by her husband, Bob Thiele. Among her collaborators were Count Basie, Duke Ellington, Dizzy Gillespie, Bobby Hackett and Earl Hines.

Before he was discovered, Dean Martin (1917–1995) bounced around the state in the bands of Walt Sears (Chillicothe), Ernie McKay (Columbus) and Sammy Watkins (Cleveland). Born Dino Crocetti in Steubenville, he first changed his name to Dino Martini before settling on Dean Martin (or just "Dino"). An all-around entertainer—actor, singer, comedian and larger-than-life personality who didn't appear to work very hard at any of them—Martin was unquestionably a pop singer, but did he sing jazz? He sang whatever he felt, and if it sometimes sounded like jazz, so be it. But he was too savvy to allow himself to be categorized as anything but a saloon singer with a comfortable baritone.

Which brings us back to this: "The dilemma of jazz singing can be expressed as a paradox: all jazz derives from vocal music, but all jazz singing is derived from instrumental music."[44] Singers want to sound like horns; horn players want to sound like singers.

7

The American Dream

On September 16, 1940, President Franklin D. Roosevelt initiated the first peacetime draft in the United States. Less than a year later, Pearl Harbor was attacked by the Japanese, and the nation went to war. During the next five years, some ten million American men between eighteen and forty-five were inducted into military service. Not surprisingly, they took their music with them.

There wasn't a camp, base or ship that didn't boast its own dance band or swing combo, often more than one. Armed Forces Radio provided regular broadcasts of swing and jazz music, many specially recorded by music's biggest names. Even the U.S. Navy School of Music got into the act, incorporating swing and jazz in its wartime curriculum.

A number of popular bandleaders, most notably a too-old-to-be-drafted Glenn Miller but also Artie Shaw, Larry Clinton and Claude Thornhill, enlisted and brought members of their bands along. As David Baker put it, "Jazz and swing were part of the American dream for which our boys were fighting."[45]

Back home, the ranks of many bands were decimated by the draft. The demand for replacement musicians provided opportunities for those too young, too old, too medically unsuitable or too female to fight. In Columbus, workers at the Curtiss-Wright Aircraft Division formed a twelve-member swing combo, a smaller jump combo, the fourteen-member Jive Bombers and a twelve-man vocal group, the Harmonaires.[46]

When World War II ended in 1945, not everyone felt like dancing. For many, it was hard to shake the horrors of combat. Much as the First World War had transformed the visual arts, the Second World War would change music, particularly classical and jazz.

For most Americans alive at the time, April 12, 1945, is forever remembered as the day President Roosevelt died. However, for a few Americans, mostly African American, it is recalled as the date of the Freeman Field Mutiny. Even though 101 African American officers were arrested at Freeman Army Airfield in southern Indiana, the mainstream media barely noticed. Their "crime" had been attempting to integrate the all-white officers' club.

The Freeman Field Mutiny was such a politically charged issue that President Harry Truman moved the all-minority 477th Composite Group to Lockbourne Field just south of Columbus in March 1946. As a result, Lockbourne also became the de facto home of the fabled Tuskegee Airmen.

More than a few citizens of Columbus weren't all that thrilled with the idea of stationing "a bunch of troublemakers" just outside the city limits.[17] However, some would come to embrace this remarkable group of men and women who could not be integrated into white units—"not only the pilots, flight officers and meteorologists, but also the black lawyers, doctors, nurses, engineers and teachers." And, as it turned out, musicians.

Chief Warrant Officer John Brice was responsible for the true miracle when he put together a 160-piece orchestra and two jazz bands, even though he was only authorized to have twenty-eight musicians altogether. Brice was determined to make the 766th Air Corps Band the equal of the all-white Army Air Corps Band in Washington, D.C. Word quickly spread that Lockbourne Air Force Base (LAFB) was the place to be for aspiring African American musicians.

Ivory "Dwike" Mitchell, a pianist, had enlisted at sixteen; Willie Ruff, a French horn player, lied about his age to join the service at fourteen. Both were still teenagers when they met at Lockbourne in 1947, and Mitchell soon gave Ruff a crash course on how to play the string bass. They would go on to form a far-reaching musical partnership that has endured more than fifty-five years.

In this conservatory-like environment, Mitchell and Ruff received a first-rate musical education. It was at Lockbourne that Mitchell was first exposed to the recordings of Toledo's Art Tatum, while Ruff started taking French horn lessons from Abe Kniaz, first chair horn player of the Columbus Philharmonic. "We were all outclassed," Ruff later recalled. "We were the youngsters of the group, and on the receiving end of the whole learning process."

Other notable musicians to come out of Lockbourne were John Coltrane's drummer, Elvin Jones (who studied with local percussion teacher Al "Rags" Anderson) and Sun Ra's tenor sax man, John Gilmore. Jones described himself as an "understudy" who "just went along to watch." Sadly, Brice's vision for the 766th came to an end in 1948 owing to his untimely death.

When returning servicemen began calling for jazz to be taught at the college level, the University of North Texas became the first institution of higher education to offer a jazz degree in 1947. A year earlier, William "Ziggy" Coyle, Paul DeFrancis, Alan Abel and Bill Cole had founded the Ohio State University Jazz Forum as "an outlet for students who performed jazz and to seriously present the product, for better or worse, to the University and the surrounding populace."

The Jazz Forum invited the Lockbourne musicians to join them for their regular jam sessions. Mitchell, in

Longtime musical partners Dwike Mitchell and Willie Ruff first got together at Lockbourne Air Force Base. *LFTJ.*

particular, became something of a local celebrity, performing on WCOL radio's weekly *Party Line* broadcasts with the sixty-five-piece LAFB band. Within two years, the Jazz Forum had attracted two thousand members and spawned its own eighteen-piece big orchestra. Interest in jazz on college campuses mushroomed to such an extent that *DownBeat* announced it would be increasing its coverage of the campus music scene.

On March 2, 1953, the Dave Brubeck Quartet recorded the landmark album *Jazz at Oberlin* in the college's Finney Chapel. Although the Oberlin Conservatory of Music was the nation's oldest, jazz was not a part of the curriculum and would not be until 1972. However, the success of Brubeck's album was, according to Professor Wendell Logan, "the watershed event that signaled the change of performance space for jazz from the nightclub to the concert hall."

Nearly thirty years earlier, in January 1924, twenty-year-old cornet soloist Bix Beiderbecke and the Wolverines were hired to play a fraternity party at Miami University in Oxford.[18] Inspired by these apostles of hot jazz, a handful of students decided to form their own band. They called themselves the Campus Owls and wrangled a booking at Cunningham's Restaurant. For the next thirty-seven years, the Campus Owls were a Miami institution, playing parties and dances locally and also hitting the road for tours of Europe, Japan, Scotland, England and Germany.

Drummer Gene Krupa, who once shared the bill with the Owls, said he didn't know of a college band that was their equal. Les Brown said the Owls were better than his Duke University band.

Among the many members of the Owls was alto saxophonist Henry "Hank Geer" Gerspacher (1922–2000), "dean of Cleveland jazz musicians," who had previously toured with the Ray Anthony Orchestra. In the late 1940s, tenor sax player Charles "Chuz" Alfred (1932–) from Lancaster attended Miami University just so he could join the Campus Owls. Herman "Duke" Jenkins (1918–2009) attended Miami with the goal of becoming a doctor but was persuaded to sing with the Owls. For many years, he led a well-known trio in Cleveland. The Owls' theme song was "Into the Night," composed by student Herbert Eidemiller.

In Columbus, pianist Richard "Dick" Cone, a member of the Ernie Wolfle Quartet, and sax man Clarence "Sonny" McBroom (1934–), a veteran of the Archie "Stomp" Gordon band, put together an orchestra in the late 1950s to play their original arrangements. When McBroom enrolled at Ohio State, the group quickly evolved into the fourteen-piece OSU Jazz Forum Big Band. Led by tenor player Lowell Latto, the ensemble competed in the inaugural Intercollegiate Jazz Festival at Notre Dame.

Established in 1959, the Notre Dame festival is the oldest collegiate jazz festival in the country. The first year, Sonny McBroom was honored as the top tenor sax player, while the band itself placed third behind groups from Minnesota and Indiana. It was one of four (out of seventeen) bands representing Ohio; the others were from the University of Cincinnati, Miami University and Oberlin College. By the following year, the Jazz Forum had appeared in its own monthly WOSU television series and released an album, *Swinging at Ohio State*. It also returned to Notre Dame, where it placed second.

In 1964, Ohio State returned with two bands: the Phi Mu Alpha Jazz Workshop led by trumpeter Riley Norris and the Ohio State University Jazz Workshop led by reedman Ladd McIntosh (1941–). Their presence heralded the start of a new era in jazz at Ohio State.

"I was at Ohio State for eleven years on and off," McIntosh recalled.

After the upstart OSU Jazz Forum Orchestra placed third at the Notre Dame Jazz Festival in 1959, the group starred in its own local TV show on WOSU and released an album. *LFTJ.*

I started my own jazz band there in '63. I ran it for five years as a student. It wasn't a course—I just had to write music…I wrote music all week long, and the band met every Sunday evening. There were times I'd drop out of school, but I kept the band. Then I started a second band, a feeder band to prepare players for the "Maynard" [Ferguson-style] band. I wrote all the music for that, too.

In addition to leading McIntosh's "feeder" band, Norris headed a popular regional band that was based in Columbus but drew its membership from many of the small towns nearby. What elevated it above many similar ensembles was the four-sax, six-brass arrangements supplied by Dick Cone. After the enigmatic Cone moved to New York City in 1970, he started a rehearsal band that was later continued by Phil Woods as the Delaware Water Gap Celebration of the Arts Festival Orchestra after Cone's death.

The OSU Jazz Workshop took home the Duke Ellington Award in 1967 as the best collegiate jazz band at the first National Intercollegiate Jazz Festival in Miami, Florida, while McIntosh was honored with the Stan Kenton Award for the best original competition. John Wilson of the *New York Times* raved, "A mere mastery of mechanics, which in past collegiate festivals might have been enough to distinguish a group, did not suffice in this instance. Originality and creativity, combined with a high performance level, were present in sufficient quantities to swing the emphasis to these aspects."

In 1970, trumpeter Thomas "Tom" Battenberg (1941–   ) from Dayton, a member of the OSU faculty, took the helm of the newly formed Ohio State University Jazz Ensemble for a twenty-year run. Continuing in the tradition of the Jazz Workshop, this band went on to win many awards and turn out many top-rank musicians. Five years later, Ohio State created a Jazz Studies Department within the School of Music. As director Joseph A. Levey noted, the curriculum was "designed to prepare the student for 'real world' music." When Battenberg left his position as conductor of the Jazz Ensemble, Dr. Ted McDaniel took his place.

Other Ohio colleges competing at Notre Dame over the years were the University of Dayton, Case Institute, Muskingum College, University of Akron, Capital University and Bowling Green State University. Both Akron and Oberlin joined Ohio State in being among the few schools to have two separate bands competing at the same time, reflecting the strength of their respective programs. Inevitably, these schools established renowned jazz studies programs as well.

At the Forty-fourth Annual Collegiate Jazz Festival in 2002, the Oberlin Jazz Ensemble earned a superior rating, with four members singled out for individual honors. As juror Rodney Whitaker put it, "Finally, a band that can play the blues." It was a fitting tribute to educator and composer Wendell Logan (1940–2010), who arrived at Oberlin in 1973, when jazz was strictly an extracurricular activity. It took him the better part of two decades to develop a jazz curriculum, culminating in the establishment of an official jazz major in 1989. Two years later, the conservatory began admitting students on the basis of jazz talent alone.

Although Oberlin had been represented at the first three jazz festivals held at Notre Dame, there had been a thirty-year break before it returned in 1991 with a jazz ensemble founded and conducted by Logan. One of his students was tenor sax player and bestselling author James McBride. A modest man, Logan refused to take credit for his achievement, insisting that he was simply the "facilitator." "You never create anything without help," he noted. "None of us is more important than the janitor."

The University of Akron Jazz Ensemble made its first appearance at the Notre Dame festival in 1979. The following year, the group performed at the prestigious Montreux Jazz Festival. It was directed by faculty member Roland Paolucci (1938–   ) and included a young trumpet player named

John A. "Jack" Schantz (1954–   ). Paolucci had founded the school's jazz studies program in 1975.

In 1972, trumpeter and educator Ray Eubanks (1941–   ), who had previously been a member of the Jazz Workshop at Ohio State, Ladd McIntosh's Live New Breed and Al Waslohn's Big Band, put together the Jazz Rock Ensemble (later Fusion Music Orchestra) at Capital University. Some of the best young talent in the city was attracted to his cutting-edge program. Four years later, Eubanks founded the jazz studies program at Capital University in Columbus. The first baccalaureate degree program in the Midwest, it numbered among its faculty Vaughn Wiester, Dave Wheeler, Byron Rooker, Cornell Wiley, Stan Smith, Bob Breithaupt and Bobby Pierce.

The Cincinnati College–Conservatory of Music was already one of the country's leading music conservatories, dating back to 1867. Pianist Claude Thornhill and trumpeter Al Hirt were some of its graduates. From 1983 to 2010, Rick VanMatre was director of the jazz studies division, which, when compared to the three-thousand-student Berklee College of Music, is "more of a boutique program," with just fifty students.

"How we prepare them is by giving them a comprehensive musical experience that allows them to thrive in a number of areas—not just performing, but technology, composition, arranging, recording, the business of music, the music industry and hitting the necessary skills about publicity, self-promotion and teaching," said Scott Belck, who replaced VanMatre upon his retirement.

While he was a student at Youngstown State University (YSU), Bill Bodine helped found the school's jazz studies program along with Tony Leonardi and Phil Wilson. In 1969, under the direction of Leonardi, the first coordinator of the program, the YSU Jazz Ensemble began to gain national recognition. It was named the "Most Outstanding Band" at the Wichita Jazz Festival in 1976 and was the first ensemble to win both the Big Band and Small Group competitions in the same year. Its recording of "Biddle de Bop" in 2000 won the *DownBeat* "College Outstanding Performance" award in the Twenty-third Annual Student Music Awards. When Leonardi died in 2001, Dr. Kent Englehardt, a former student of his, was hired as his replacement.

Over the last half century, nearly every university and college in Ohio (and many high schools, as well) have taken steps to include jazz in their music curriculums.

8
Looking Backward

By the 1940s, some jazz musicians were already looking back to the music's formative years and attempting to re-create the earlier New Orleans–style "hot" jazz sound—only now it was being called "Dixieland," a term that is also widely disparaged. Leonard Bernstein, in *The Joy of Music* (1959), wrote, "One of the most exhilarating sounds in all music is that of a Dixieland band blaring out its final chorus, all stops out, with everyone improvising together." Many agree.

For years, Mount Healthy–born, Bexley-raised Walter "Pee Wee" Hunt was the featured trombonist and novelty vocalist of the famed Casa Loma Orchestra, which he co-founded. He left the band in 1943 and not long afterward joined the Merchant Marines. During the war, Hunt put together a small combo and continued to perform with it when he left the service. While working with a group of studio musicians in 1948, he recorded a hokey version of "Twelfth Street Rag," originally composed in 1914. It became an immediate sensation, selling more than three million copies.

"The Happy Man of Dixieland," as Hunt came to be billed, quickly assembled a touring unit and hit the road. In 1953, another reworking of an old chestnut—"Oh!"—also became a sizable hit. For a decade, Hunt was in the forefront of the Dixieland or Trad Jazz Revival. The difference was that while groups led by Bob Crosby, Eddie Condon, Wild Bill Davison, Max Kaminsky and even Louis Armstrong were serious practitioners of the genre, Hunt's approach was strictly tongue-in-cheek.

On one side were the guys in the straw hats and sleeve garters who played "goodtime" music, often in pizza parlors or faux Gay Nineties saloons. On the other were the apostles of "hot jazz" who, dismayed by the cool jazz and bop movements, were seeking to return the music to its (New Orleans) roots. Many of the musicians on both sides were from the Midwest, and some of the best were from Ohio. From a commercial standpoint, Dixieland is the most popular form of jazz since the swing era. The Dukes of Dixieland alone released several dozen albums on the way to becoming a household name.

When it comes to trad, or traditional, jazz, there have been few people more devoted to its revival than Gene Mayl', a four-valve tuba player from Dayton. In 1946, he put together the original incarnation of the Dixieland Rhythm Kings with cornetist Carl Halen (1928–) while they were both still teenagers. They took as their role models Armstrong's Hot Fives and Hot Sevens and Jelly Roll Morton's Red Hot Peppers. After a sojourn in Paris, Mayl returned to Dayton in 1949, put the band back together and began touring.

By the time he cut a self-titled album on the Riverside label in 1953, Mayl was using all session players. However, Halen, from Hamilton, had assembled most of the original members and was laying down tracks in Yellow Springs as the Gin Bottle Seven. This group would go on to release a couple albums with Riverside as well, in 1955 and 1957.

When the Dixieland Rhythm Kings performed at a jazz festival in Columbus in 1954, they shared the stage with George Lewis, the Saints & Sinners and pianist Ralph Sutton, all veteran players. The same year, the band went to New Orleans "to fulfill an ill-advised booking in the Dream Room on Bourbon Street, an upholstered sewer run by characters that shouldn't have had a license," according to Al Rose. "Many native jazz bands were working the street in those years, but they'd become stereotyped and lazy, playing a handful of tired tunes too fast and too loud."[49]

Although they did not get a good reception, Rose "found their performance fascinating, exciting, and extremely professional." He promptly booked them for a jazz club concert, where they were acclaimed by two thousand jazz lovers as the best band "in the concert, in the city, and maybe in the country."

In 1953, old-time musician George Lewis and his band had been invited by the Miami Folk Arts Society to play concerts at Miami University and the University of Cincinnati. With a repertoire ranging from New Orleans funeral marches to Mardi Gras parade tunes, Lewis was an enormous hit—proclaimed the best musical attraction to grace college campuses in twenty years. The following year, Lewis returned to the Buckeye state to record a live album at the Ohio State University, *Jass at the Ohio Union* (1954). While the playing was somewhat uneven, Lewis was hailed as the "real thing" in contrast to the more commercial forms of Dixieland that were taking hold.

Four years earlier, Harry Epp of Columbus had put together the Columbus Rhythm Kings in emulation of Mayl's group. Although Epp knew his way around the piano, what he really excelled at was the banjo. A decade later, the group was known as Harry Epp and His Muskat Ramblers when working major clubs throughout the Midwest and Canada. Epp would later work with Frank Hubbell's Stompers and Eddie Bayard's band on the *Mississippi Queen*. One early member of the band was trumpeter John Henry "Johnny" Windhurst. Another was cornetist Dick Baars (1935–1971), from Columbus, who worked in Ed Reed's Riverboat Five before taking over "Pee Wee" Hunt's band, which he renamed the Slabtown Marching Society.

Saints & Sinners was an all-star group assembled by Columbus promoter Lou Posey in 1954. In addition to Windhurst, members included such luminaries as trumpeter Buck Clayton, pianist Al Waslohn (unknown–1977), pianist Joe Sullivan, trombonist Russell "Big Chief" Moore, drummer Barrett Deems (1914–1988) and trumpeter Napoleon "Nappy" Trotter. Waslohn, Windhurst and Deems (the man who "makes coffee nervous," per Louis Armstrong) were all Columbus residents during this period, with Deems offering drum lessons to a lucky few.

One of the premier Dixieland combos of the 1950s and 1960s, the Salt City Six was founded in 1952 by clarinetist Jack Maheu, a recent graduate

Tom Swisher plays the drums behind the front line of the highly regarded Salt City Six. *Tom Swisher.*

of the Syracuse University School of Music. Considered musically superior to the better-known Dukes of Dixieland, the band had a veritable who's who of Ohio musicians during its seventeen-year history. Among its 132 members were trumpeters Wild Bill Davison* and Dick Baars, pianist John Ulrich*, drummers Glen Kimmel (1939–2006) and Tom Swisher (1944–   ) and bassist Gene Mayl*.

Toledo's Cakewalkin' Jass Band was organized in December 1967 by clarinetist Ray Heitger (1943–   ) and settled into a long run at Tony Packo's Café. Originally a four-piece group (banjo, drums, piano and clarinet), it slowly doubled in size. Over the years, there have been twenty-seven regulars and another twenty-seven or so substitute players. The band prides itself on its repertoire of more than 470 authentic New Orleans–style songs. A reviewer in the *Mississippi Rag* noted that the band "has a magnetism that both derives from and also transcends the appeal of traditional jazz."

Cincinnati's Queen City Jazz Band was founded by trombonist/vocalist Monte Tabbert in the 1950s. It included Mathias Fuchs from Hamilton, a veteran of Carl Halen's Gin Bottle Seven, whose piano playing actually improved after he lost two fingers in an industrial accident. Other members were Phil Stikeleather (tuba), Frank Powers (reeds) and Dave Train (banjo/ ukulele). In 1967, Tabbert died in an automobile accident at the age of thirty-two.

Classic jazz clarinet and tenor sax player Frank Powers (1931–2002) was born in Akron. An architect by trade, Powers pursued his interest in jazz by playing on weekends and recording with such groups as the Queen City Jazz Band, the Dixieland Rhythm Kings and the Gin Bottle Seven.

Waldo's Gutbucket Syncopators was formed in 1970 during a phone conversation between Powers and pianist Terry Waldo (1944–   ) to explore America's musical heritage, specifically blues, ragtime, jazz, stomps and early show tunes. Waldo was starting to make a name for himself in the ragtime revivalist world; Powers had already been there and done that. Up until then, Waldo had been performing solo or in a duo with vocalist Susan LaMarche around central Ohio. With Powers, Roy "Swine-Chops" Tate (trumpet) and Bob Butters (trombone) from the Queen City Jazz Band and Gene Mayl's Dixieland Rhythm Kings, plus a few others, he put together the Syncopators.

Born in Ironton, Waldo grew up in Columbus. His neighbor was John Baker, who owned a vast collection of early jazz recordings, films and piano rolls (now housed at the American Jazz Museum in Kansas City), which spurred Waldo's interest in ragtime music. In 1969, Waldo met Eubie Blake,

A poster from ragtime
pianist and historian
Terry Waldo's 1975
concert tour. *Terry
Waldo.*

Noble Sissle's one-time partner and a living relic of the era, who took him
under his wing. Five years later, he produced a twenty-six-part series for
National Public Radio entitled *This Is Ragtime* that led to a book of the
same name (1976, updated 1991, 2009). He has since gone on to produce
over forty albums and many scores for theater, as well as providing ragtime
instruction at Jazz at Lincoln Center in New York City.

The Capital City Jazz Band started around 1980 to play at the Dell
Restaurant in Columbus but soon moved over to Deibel's. It included many
veterans of Al Waslohn's various bands. Banjoist/vocalist Hank Harding
was a good friend of trumpeter Bobby Hackett and had played with many
big names in jazz.

The High Street Stompers was organized by Tom Battenberg, director of the
OSU Jazz Ensemble, in 1987. Originally, it consisted entirely of music faculty
from Ohio State and was a vehicle for letting off steam. Their goal was to play
early 1900 New Orleans "jass" exactly the way it was originally recorded.

Columbus's long-running Toll House Jazz Band was founded in 1989 by banjo player Mike Evans. Specialists in "hot jazz" à la King Oliver and Jelly Roll Morton, the ensemble has included some outstanding instrumentalists over the years. Joe Lord toured with Tex Benecke, played lead clarinet with the Longine Symphonette and was principal flutist with the Leningrad Ballet. For churches, the group performs under the name the Dixie Saints.

Cincinnati's Buffalo Ridge Jazz Band is one of the most popular acts on the "hot" jazz circuit. Formed in 1984 by banjo player and vocalist Mike Adams, the group holds down a regular gig at the Dee Felice Café in Covington, Kentucky. Felice was a veteran of the Ralph Marterie Orchestra but turned down an opportunity to play with Lawrence Welk in order to start his own Dixieland combo with Carl Halen, Frank Powers and others. "It's a disease, you know," Felice said. "Playing music, that is. You make a poor living at it at best. But it gets a hold of you. You can't give it up."

Adams is a veteran of the New Orleans–based Ragtimers, Your Father's Mustache Show Band and the Banjo Kings at Disney World. Bob Butters, a longtime Columbus resident, joined a dozen years later. In the 1946 *Look* magazine swing band contest at Carnegie Hall, Butters carried off the Tommy Dorsey trophy for his trombone playing. While a member of the house band at Boston's Savoy Café, he had the opportunity to play behind such jazz legends as Wild Bill Davison, Henry "Red" Allen, Max Kaminsky and others. After moving to Ohio in 1951, he worked with Carl Halen's Gin Bottle Seven, Eddie Bayard's Bourbon Street Five, Gene Mayl's Dixieland Rhythm Kings and Terry Waldo's Gutbucket Syncopators.

Perhaps the mission statement of the Central Ohio Hot Jazz Society says it best: "There are many names for 'Our Kind of Music': Dixieland, TRAD jazz, hot jazz, early jazz, even 'jass.' Whatever you want to call it, we love it!"

9
Enter the Atomic Age

A tune from 1949 sets the stage for the beginning of the 1950s: "BeBop Spoken Here."

Bop was jittery, slashing, unsettling, even dangerous. It was a reflection of the unsettled state of the world coming out of the war. And when hard bop couldn't say what some musicians were feeling, "free jazz" erupted, almost as a mind-clearing to pop music. However, within a few years a more relaxed, peaceful and meandering style emerged that came to be called "cool." Something else was happening, too. Stan Kenton had arrived with what he called "progressive jazz." It was still a big band, but the music was no longer danceable. The audience was expected to simply stand—or sit—and watch the musicians play.

At the beginning of the decade, trains, automobiles and buses were still the most common modes of transportation. Air travel remained a luxury, reserved for the few musicians who could afford to "live large." Big band swing was still popular on the radio and recordings (although less so). But many of the big bands were breaking up because they could not compete with "free" entertainment on the television.

In June 1953, Lou Wilson, owner of the Carolyn Nite Club, hired Rusty Bryant and his band for a limited engagement, thereby setting in motion a series of events that would forever change the history of music in Columbus. At that point, the tenor saxophonist had been working around town, trying to generate some excitement with his own combos, but he always wound up working for someone else. He was replacing Wendell Hawkins and His Night Hawks, who had just finished a year's stay—a club record. (Hawkins would later record an extremely rare album, *Mr. Hawkins at the Piano* (1961), for King Records.)

Between stints with Rusty Bryant, Chuz Alfred and Lou Donaldson, guitarist Warren Stephens opened the first jazz coffeehouse in Columbus, the Sacred Mushroom. *Chuz Alfred.*

Billed as "Mr. Sax," Bryant was joined by Jimmy "Stix" Rogers (drums)[50] and Fred Smith (bass). Hawkins was brought back so Wilson could advertise that he had two bands in one, but Bryant soon left no doubts that it was his gig. He had taken the Jimmy Forrest tune "Night Train" and energized it by doubling the tempo. It became their most requested number, so Bryant pressed a few copies (backed with "Castle Rock") on the Carolyn label for the fans. Meanwhile, Hank Marr had replaced Hawkins, and guitarist Warren Stephens was added.

Pushed by deejays in Columbus, Cleveland and Springfield, the record quickly became a regional hit and was picked up by Dot Records, which rereleased it as "All Nite Long." When it began breaking big in Chicago, Pittsburgh, Atlanta, Milwaukee and Detroit, offers for the band started rolling in from Philadelphia to Las Vegas. Bryant soon took his band on the road, so Wilson hired his brother, pianist/saxophonist Paul "Dusty" Bryant, to fill in for him at the Carolyn Club and perform his material.

In August 1954, the Rusty Bryant band joined the "Rhythm and Blues Show," along with the Drifters, the Spaniels, LaVern Baker, King Pleasure,

Erskine Hawkins, Roy Hamilton and others, for a series of one-nighters. According to Robert Pruter in *Goldmine*, "This tour was highly instrumental in helping to break rhythm 'n' blues into the white market as rock 'n' roll music." More than 9,400 fans showed up in Cleveland, where the show was promoted by deejay Alan Freed. By the following August, "Night Train/ All Nite Long" had sold an estimated 700,000 copies and had become the anthem for a generation.

Two years earlier, Bryant had played for a talent show at Beatty Recreation Center just for the exposure. About six hundred people came out to see his band, vocalist Duke Brooks and "the teenage tenor sax sensation" Ronnie Kirk. The future Rahsaan Roland Kirk⁔ asked him for lessons, but Bryant admitted there wasn't much he could teach the kid. In 1956, Kirk recorded his extremely rare debut album, *Triple Threat*, for King Records, on which he demonstrated his ability to play multiple wind instruments simultaneously.

Bryant also had a great influence on Grover Washington Jr. (1943–1999), who was playing with the Four Clefs, a Columbus-based traveling band. Fresh out of high school and told he was too young to enter the clubs, he would sit outside to listen to Rusty wail. "He taught me to be a complete musician," Washington recalled. "[S]howed me fingerings and spacing's…Rusty would say music is like fine wine; it has to breathe, too…even silence is a part of music."

Although it was Bryant's band, not everyone came out to see the tenor sax giant walk-the-bar, blow smoke rings from his horn or play while lying on a bearskin rug. Hank Marr, who had switched to organ, was also attracting his share of fans, and one of them was pianist Don Patterson⁔. Marr, who had also started on piano, gave the young man his first chance to play the Hammond B-3 at the Club Regal. He was hooked immediately but didn't debut on the instrument in 1959. A long partnership with saxophonist Sonny Stitt firmly established him as an original voice on the organ.

After Lancaster-born Charles "Chuz" Alfred left Miami University, he waded into the local club scene, fronting his own combo. A dynamic tenor player, Alfred quickly forged a musical partnership with trombonist Ola Hanson (1932–2009) from Canton, with whom he released an album on the Savoy label, *Jazz Young Bloods* (1955). They spent the 1950s playing all over the East Coast, Midwest and into Canada before Hanson left to tour and record with the Kai Winding Septet, and Alfred did the same with the Ralph Marterie Orchestra. Plans for a joint Chuz Alfred–Rusty Bryant super band fell through at the last minute when Bryant took another job.

However, Bryant did briefly hook up with pianist Stomp Gordon⁔ for a band they called the All-Stars in 1957. It included Dick Smith (bass) and

Two of the hottest tenors in town, Rusty Bryant and Chuz Alfred, planned to battle it out every night in a combined band, circa 1957. *Chuz Alfred.*

Charles Crosby (drums). This band quickly broke up. Crosby, who had come to Columbus four years earlier when he left B.B. King, had been living at the Club Regal, where he booked the music. He also played with Chuz Alfred before going on tour with Rahsaan Roland Kirk in the 1960s.

Down in southwestern Ohio ("Midwestern Hayride" country), a lot was happening musically, especially with country and western, rhythm and blues and early rock-and-roll. King Records, founded by Syd Nathan in 1943, was a Cincinnati-based recording label. It started out focused on the "hillbilly" market ("If it's a King, It's a Hillbilly—If it's a Hillbilly, it's a King"). In late 1950, it added its Federal subsidiary to record such acts as James Brown and Hank Ballard and the Midnighters. It also dabbled in jazz but didn't know much what to do with it.

King not only used a lot of local talent (the Queen City became a mecca for southern musicians) but also took advantage of the artists traveling through the Tri-State region. It was a very streamlined operation, with everything done at one location. This enabled it to produce smaller record runs just for

In 1958, Dale Wright & the Rock-Its recorded "She's Neat" at King Studios, and the song peaked at number thirty-eight on the *Billboard* Hot 100. *Randy McNutt.*

radio stations in the hope of garnering airplay (which makes some extremely rare). In 1955, Zanesville's Albert "Andy Gibson" (1913–1961) joined King Records as music director from 1955 to 1960. Previously, he had worked with Count Basie, Duke Ellington and Harry James.

Guitarist Cal Collins (1933–2001) was just getting his start in the early 1950s. Influenced by the guitar stylings of Irving Ashby and John Collins, he established a solid reputation in Ohio and Indiana during the next couple of decades, working with Hank Marr and others, before Benny Goodman "discovered" him in 1976. During the three years he spent with Goodman, he was house guitarist at Concord Records and made numerous recordings, including his own *Cincinnati to LA* (1978) and *Ohio Style* (1991).

The Modern Jazz Disciples, whose members included drummer Roy McCurdy (1933–2008), bassist Lee Tucker (1933–), William Brown (1934–), normaphone/euphonium[51] player William "Hicky" Kelley (1929–) and alto saxophonist Curtis Peagler (1930–1992), was a bop group formed in 1958. Peagler, Kelley and Tucker were all Cincinnati natives who got together while

For many years, jazz guitarist Cal Collins cast a long shadow in the Cincinnati music scene. *LFTJ.*

attending the University of Cincinnati. Taking up residence as the house band at Babe Baker's Club, they were heard by Eddie "Lockjaw" Davis. He had them cut a demo, and they were quickly signed to Prestige's New Jazz label.

The band's self-titled debut earned it a four-and-a-half-star review in *DownBeat*, but sales were sluggish. For its second album, Wilbur "Slim" Jackson replaced McCurdy. And then the band broke up in 1961, with Peagler going on to work with Ray Charles, Count Basie and the San Diego–based Sweet Baby Blues Band. He later released a solo album, *I'll Be Around* (1988). McCurdy, nicknamed "Whitefolks" by Sonny Stitt, went on to play with Cannonball Adderley, Rahsaan Roland Kirk and Ben Webster. He was a member of Wee Three with Cal Collins and bassist Michael Moore and longtime house drummer at the Dee Felice Café.

Television turned out to be a boon to many Ohio musicians, especially those from the northern part of the state. Cleveland's Henry Mancini first made a name for himself during the 1950s for numerous TV and film scores, including the jazz-infused themes for *Mr. Lucky* and *Peter Gunn*. In fact, the music from these popular television shows was the first exposure to jazz for a whole generation of future musicians.

Anthony Renaldo (1915–   ) was an Akron clarinet player who adopted the professional name of Tommy Reynolds. After attending the University of Akron, he landed a job with Isham Jones, but a year or two later he put together his own band. Throughout the 1940s and into the 1950s, Reynolds continued to tour and play major ballrooms and theaters in New York and Chicago but never quite got his big break. During the mid-1950s, he became music director at WOR in New York City, where he produced the long-running program *Bandstand U.S.A.*

Trumpeter Ray Anthony (1922–   ) grew up in Cleveland. In 1941, he joined the Glenn Miller Band and appeared in the movie *Sun Valley Serenade*, but then he left to join Jimmy Dorsey. Following World War II, Anthony formed his own group. With movie star good looks and a trumpet sound like Harry James, he turned out a string of hits: "The Bunny Hop," "Hokey Pokey" and "Dragnet Theme" (all in 1953). Considered one of the more adventuresome of the big band leaders, he was immortalized in the song "Opus No. 1" (1944), in which the Mills Brothers sing, "It's not for Sammy Kaye, hey, hey, hey," but hoped Anthony would "rock it."

Born Ralph Elias Flennken in Lorain, Ralph Flanagan (1914–1995) contributed arrangements to the bands of Sammy Kaye, Blue Barron and Alvino Rey, in addition to leading his own band. After serving in the

An exuberant Ray Anthony "rocking it" for his fans in New York City, 1947. *WG-LOC.*

Merchant Marines during World War II, he was signed by Glenn Miller's last A&R man, who encouraged him to adopt the "Miller sound." By 1951, Flanagan had the number one big band in the country according to several polls, including *Billboard*. He enjoyed great success with such songs as "Hot Toddy" (1953) and "Flanagan's Boogie" (1955).

On hundreds of TV shows during the 1950s and 1960s, the title card read, "Music by DeVol." Frank DeVol (1911–1999) grew up in Canton, the son of a local bandleader. In the 1930s, he joined Horace Heidt as an arranger before moving on to the Alvino Rey Orchestra. From the 1940s on, DeVol was a highly sought-after arranger who had a number one hit with Nat King Cole's "Nature Boy" (1948) for Capitol Records. As a result, he was promptly hired at rival Columbia Records, for which he recorded a series of "mood music" albums as "Music by DeVol" and also scored many movies and TV shows.

After the war, Cleveland's Ernie Freeman (1922–1981) headed for Los Angeles to try to break into the music business. It was tough going at first. Then he was hired to improve the musical quality of the popular B. Bumble and the Stingers. His R&B hit "Jivin' O' Round" (1955) led to a job with Imperial Records, where he is rumored to have played piano on Fats Domino's hits. In 1966, he was hired as musical director for Frank Sinatra's Reprise label. He subsequently won Grammys for the albums *Strangers in the Night* (1966) and *Bridge Over Troubled Water* (1970).

Taking a somewhat different route, composer and conductor Artie Kane (1929–   ), born Aaron Cohen, was a child prodigy in Columbus, starting out with the famous Columbus Boychoir. After performing "Rhapsody in Blue" with Izler Solomon and the Columbus Philharmonic, he went on the road for ten years, including a stint with singer Jaye P. Morgan. Eventually, Kane landed in Hollywood, where he was hired by Dominic Frontiere as first-call pianist at MGM studios and championed by fellow Buckeye Henry Mancini. With Ralph Grierson, he recorded *Gershwin 'S Wonderful* (1976), a Grammy nominated twin-piano album. He also composed jazz-oriented music for numerous TV shows and several movies.

Although best known for his classical work, clarinetist Richard Stoltzman (1942–   ) also plays jazz on occasion, as evidenced by his album *New York Counterpoint* (1985). The two-time Grammy Award winner was born in Nebraska but grew up in Cincinnati and attended college at Ohio State, where he worked in several local combos, including one with Ray Eubanks. He has performed with Gary Burton, Chick Corea, Eddie Gomez, Keith Jarrett, George Shearing, Wayne Shorter and Mel Tormé, as well as other jazz stars.

Composer/arranger/bandleader Al Waslohn set the standard for music on pioneering television broadcasts in Ohio. *LFTJ.*

Columbus station WBNS-TV decided the time was ripe for a big band show. So in 1961, Al Waslohn assembled a twelve-piece group, using the best musicians available, including trumpeter Phil Sunkel (1925–   ), a Zanesville native who had worked with Charlie Barnett, Stan Getz, Sauter-Finegan, Gerry Mulligan and Gil Evans.

Originally from Oil City, Pennsylvania, pianist/arranger Waslohn had studied under Iturbe, Reiner, Stravinsky, Kostelanetz and Bernstein. After working with Buddy Morrow, Ray Anthony, Jimmy Dorsey and Buck Clayton, he settled in Columbus, where he led bands on local television starting in the early 1950s before becoming chief arranger at AVCO Broadcasting in Cincinnati. Unfortunately, the hour-long broadcasts were given a Saturday afternoon time slot opposite, of all things, Ohio State football. The show was yanked after thirteen weeks; however, Waslohn's arrangements, especially "Hungover Square," have stood the test of time.

10

Days of Turmoil
and Ferment

One of the oldest-running musical festivals in North America, the Ohio Valley Jazz Festival, as it was originally known, was founded in 1962 by Dino Santangelo strictly as a jazz concert. Over the years, the venue changed from the Carthage Fairgrounds to Paul Brown Stadium, with other stops in between. For a time, it was called the Cincinnati Jazz Festival, but it is currently the Macy's Music Festival in recognition of its corporate sponsor. The title reflects the expansion of the original concept to include not just jazz but also soul, rhythm and blues and hip-hop—contemporary music.

There are people who want jazz to stand still and always be what it was at some particular point in time. But like all organic things, jazz must grow—or die. And in the 1950s, jazz did a lot of growing. Bebop had become hard bop with the mixing in of R&B, gospel and blues. Those who preferred a softer and lighter touch spun off as "cool jazz." And a brave few tried to fly with something called "free jazz."

Several Ohioans were present at the "birth of the cool." As a child in Marion, Gerald "Gerry" Mulligan (1927–1996) was first exposed to African American musicians while hanging out at the home of his nanny, Lily Rose, who took many of them in when they were passing through town. A leading baritone saxophonist, Mulligan became famous for his soft phrasings in groups with Miles Davis and Chet Baker.

An arranger for the Dizzy Gillespie Band, Clevelander Tadd Dameron⁎ was the first to incorporate "cool jazz" into his charts. Meanwhile, Dayton flutist Bud Shank⁎, a veteran of the Stan Kenton band, quickly established himself as the embodiment of West Coast "cool" (and a much sought-after session player) when he set up shop in California.

The roots of "free jazz" are firmly planted in Ohio. Cincinnati's George Russell was the theoretician, while Cleveland's Albert Ayler[*] was the mad scientist. They introduced a style of playing that was characterized by openness to all influences and a freedom from all rules. Tonality, meter, symmetry—all the elements that traditionally distinguished music from noise—seemingly went out the window. They were replaced by an intensity of playing that bordered on religious ecstasy. Improvisation trumped everything.

Many listeners hated it, but some saw Ayler's music as an important breakthrough in the search for musical expression. He was joined in his experiments by some fellow Buckeyes. Call Cobbs Jr. (1910–1971) was a jazz pianist, electric harpsichordist and organist from Springfield. Acting as Ayler's music director (1964–70), he accompanied him live and on recordings. Later, Cobbs worked with Billie Holiday, Wardell Gray and Johnny Hodges.

Charles Tyler (1941–1992) began playing baritone and alto sax with Ayler in their hometown in the early 1960s and followed him to New York City. In addition to performing on Ayler's albums *Bells* and *Spirits Rejoice* (both 1965), he debuted as a front man of the Charles Tyler Ensemble on his own 1966 release. Pianist Bobby Few (1935–   ), from Shaker Heights, was Ayler's friend from high school and later recorded with him. Few has also worked and recorded with Archie Shepp, Alan Silva, Brook Benton, Steve Lacy, Booker Ervin and Noah Howard.

The proponents of free jazz soon found other elements to replace those they had cast off. Saxophonist Ornette Coleman developed his own theory of harmonics, which he called "harmolodics." His best-known disciple, guitarist James "Blood" Ulmer (1942–   ), has acknowledged that he obtained his jazz education in Columbus during the 1960s, when he played in Hank Marr's band. Ulmer later took up "free funk," inspired by Ayler's 1968 release, *New Grass*, which mixed rhythm and blues with free jazz. "Jazz is teacher," Ulmer famously noted. "Funk is the preacher."

Historian, scholar and critic Willard Jenkins began writing for the *Cleveland Plain Dealer* in the early 1970s and serves as editor and coordinator of the national Lost Jazz Shrines project. He has said that the city's importance in jazz history is "because it has been a stop on the so-called jazz 'circuit' of clubs and venues." As Joe Mossbrook's ongoing chronicles of jazz illustrate, the North Coast has hosted nearly all of the greats and near-greats, both on their way up and their way down. But much the same can be said for the state as a whole.

When it came to innovation, Rahsaan Roland Kirk[*] took a backseat to nobody. Visually challenged, he more than made up for his sightlessness by embracing the musical potential in all the sounds that enveloped him.[52] His music came from the heart and involved the imaginative use of handmade and repurposed instruments, often playing three at once. Kirk developed "circular breathing" (in through his nose, out through his mouth) as a way to hold a sustained note, or group of sounds, without interruption. Among his many recordings are *Does Your House Have Lions* (1961), *The Inflated Tear* (1968), *Volunteered Slavery* (1969) and *Bright Moments* (1970).

While a student at the Ohio State School for the Blind, organist Eddie Baccus Sr. (1936–   ) was recruited by Kirk, his schoolmate, to join him in a touring trio, Three Blind Mice, with drummer George Cook (also blind). Soon afterward, Kirk arranged for Baccus to record his debut album, *Feel Real* (1962).[53] For much of his career, Baccus has been keeping the jazz flame alive in his adopted hometown of Cleveland.

Todd Barkan, director of programming at Dizzy's Club Coca-Cola at Lincoln Center, grew up in Columbus. He identifies Kirk (in his pre-Rahsaan days) as having been his mentor. They spent hundreds of hours poring through stacks of records together, and Kirk would have him read him the liner notes aloud. Barkan also took piano lessons from Don Patterson and was friends with guitarist Warren Stephens, singer Nancy Wilson and saxophonist Grover Washington Jr., all of whom were very active in the local music scene at the time.

A candid shot of Ramsey Lewis, Nancy Wilson and Hank Marr (at the keyboards), back when things were just starting to happen for all of them. *LFTJ.*

Drummer Sonny Brown (1936–   ), a native of Cincinnati, played on the 1960 album *Introducing Roland Kirk* and continued to work and record with Kirk for many years afterward. Brown also worked with Frank Foster, Kenny Burrell, Coleman Hawkins and Charles Mingus. In 1968, he co-composed an opera for the New York Bass Violin Choir. Self-taught drummer Bobby Scott, also from Cincinnati, worked with Kirk, as well as Johnny Hartman, Eddie "Cleanhead" Vinson, Jimmy Forrest and Big Maybelle.

During the 1960s, Hank Marr coaxed his Hammond B3 with its Leslie speakers to the limits. He was signed to King Records in 1961, producing a series of six albums, including the legendary *Live at the 502* (1964), which reunited him with Rusty Bryant and included his hit single, "Greasy Spoon." James "Blood" Ulmer plays on *Live from the Marr-Ket Place* (1967), recorded the same year.

The founder of Strata-East Records (1971), Stanley Cowell (1941–   ) is a Toledo native who played piano with Rahsaan Roland Kirk while studying at the Oberlin Conservatory of Music. Later, he performed with Marion Brown, Max Roach, Clifford Jordan, Sonny Rollins and Stan Getz. From 1965 to 1966, he was a member of the Detroit Artist's Workshop Jazz Ensemble and co-founded Collective Black Artists, Inc., with Charles Tolliver.

A typical experience for a jazz musician during this period was that of Bobby Pierce. In 1963, he was playing piano in his own trio three nights a week in Columbus. However, with the advent of the Beatles, the demand for jazz dried up for a time, and he was forced to look elsewhere for work. Moving to New York City, Pierce worked with Gene Ammons, Sonny Stitt and James Moody on the "Chittlin' Circuit," perfecting the organ sound local hero Don Patterson had turned him onto. In 1972, he released his debut album, *Introducing Bobby Pierce*, followed by *New York* two years later. It would be another thirty-four years before he was rediscovered by Hammond B3 fanatic Pete Fallico, who produced the album *Bobby's Back* (2008).

In the late 1960s, rock bands began adding horn sections à la Blood, Sweat and Tears, while jazz combos began incorporating more of a rock sound. Such jazz-rock or fusion combos led to the crossover success of Miles Davis with his bestselling album, *Bitches Brew* (1970). The interplay between the musicians in fusion groups became so complex that Joe Zawinul of Weather Report said, "In this group, either nobody plays solo, or we all solo at the same time."

For a couple years in the late 1960s, Ladd McIntosh, fresh off the success of the award-winning Ohio State University Jazz Workshop, led the ten-piece Live New Breed. Playing his original compositions, it could hold its own with any other horn band on the scene. However, when the local

Rhodes Brothers asked Live New Breed to join them at their newly built Florida supper club, it was an offer the band couldn't refuse.

Many other players were also going on the road. Double bass player/composer Bob Cunningham (1934–   ) left Cleveland for New York City in 1960. The following year, he played at the Monterey Jazz Festival and recorded with Eric Dolphy and Bill Hardman. Throughout the 1960s, Cunningham performed on recordings with Ken McIntyre, Frank Foster and Freddie Hubbard, eventually joining Yusef Lateef in 1970.

Self-taught drummer Morey Feld (1915–1971) rose from Cleveland to play with some of the best-known bands in the business: Ben Pollack (1936), Benny Goodman (1943–1945), Eddie Condon (1946), Bobby Hackett and Billy Butterfield. He also recorded with Dizzy Gillespie, Sarah Vaughn, Ella Fitzgerald, Wild Bill Davison and Stan Getz before starting his own school for drummers in 1966. Two years later, he joined the World's Greatest Jazz Band.

Soon after graduating from college, composer and pianist Mike Longo (1939–   ) from Cincinnati was playing at the famed Metropole. Dizzy Gillespie happened to be playing upstairs, and every time he wanted to take a break, he had to pass the band playing downstairs on the way out. Longo eventually became musical director for the Dizzy Gillespie Quintet, and later Gillespie chose him to be the pianist for the Dizzy Gillespie All-Star Band. In the 1960s, Longo began to lead the Mike Longo Trio, which would remain active for the next forty-two years.

Toledo-born Ike Stubblefield (1952–   ) began playing the piano by ear from the time he was a toddler. However, he is best known for his mastery of the Hammond B3 organ. His talents were first put on display in 1968, when he backed the touring Motown Review. Soon, he was working with George Benson, B.B. King, Bobby Caldwell, Eric Clapton, Curtis Mayfield and other big names. From 1976 to 1988, Stubblefield was a studio musician for Quincy Jones, Phil Spector and Wendy Waldman.

Cleveland's Ernest Harold "Benny" Bailey (1925–2005) spent much of his career overseas. Although he started on flute, he switched to trumpet after hearing Louis Armstrong and Roy Eldridge. In 1944, Scatman Crothers took him to California. He later joined Dizzy Gillespie and Lionel Hampton for tours of Europe. While with Hampton, Quincy Jones composed "Meet Benny Bailey" (1959) in his honor. Jon Hendricks later wrote vocalese lyrics to match Bailey's trumpet solo: "Have you met Benny Bailey? Well, he's a fella that you should know."

Composer/arranger/saxophonist Willie Smith (1926–2011) grew up down the street from Benny Bailey. The two of them had gone to California with Scatman Crothers in 1945. Three years later, they joined the Lionel Hampton Orchestra; while Bailey played in the group, Smith arranged and composed. During the 1960s, Smith worked for Motown Records as a writer. After seven years, he returned to Cleveland and formed his Little Big Band. The highlight of his career occurred when Joe Lovano recorded some of his arrangements, and the album won a Grammy Award.

Blind since birth, Robert "Bob Allen" Prahin (1940–   ) began studying piano as a child in Cleveland. After attending Capital University in Columbus, he remained in Columbus to teach and perform in his long-running trio, which had a twenty-year engagement at the Christopher Inn. Allen has recorded a number of albums, including *The Naked Piano*, which featured the then new Baldwin SD-10 concert grand.

Guitarist Kenny Poole (1947–2006) was a legend in Cincinnati. He started playing "corny old tunes" at fourteen but soon moved on to jazz standards, skipping rock-and-roll entirely. During his career, Poole showcased his talent with the likes of Richard "Groove" Holmes, James Brown, Joe Pass, Herb Ellis, Chuck Mangione, Jack McDuff and Sonny Stitt.

During the decade, drummer Nick Ceroli (1939–1985) out of Warren was working with Ray Anthony, Debbie Reynolds, Lionel Hampton, Terry Gibbs and Stan Kenton. He played at the Monterey Jazz Festival (1963) and was a member of the Tijuana Brass (1965).

Whether "cool," "free," "free funk," "jazz-rock" or "fusion," the 1960s gave artists a much richer palette of sounds to work with. And with such new instruments as amplified sitars and synthesizers, musicians had greater flexibility than ever before as they moved forward. The decade also saw a proliferation of Jazz Service Organizations, feeding the continued interest in the genre. Originally geared around "hot" or "Dixieland," the preservation movement eventually grew to encompass contemporary jazz styles as well. The Northeast Ohio Jazz Society, Columbus Jazz Society, Jazz Arts Group and Dayton's City Folk were just a few organizations that began tirelessly working to collect, preserve and present the jazz heritage of their locales.

11
The Darkness Before the Dawn

Even as the "ghost bands" of Glenn Miller, Tommy Dorsey, Les Elgart, etc.,[54] were touring with old "books" from long-gone bandleaders of note, others were mixing bop with neo-swing and cool jazz, creating entirely new sounds, some charted and some made up on the spot. And a few more were returning to hot jazz. But in addition to music, there was something else in the air: social activism.

Building on the advances made in civil rights during the previous decade, Rahsaan Roland Kirk♪ founded the Jazz and Peoples Movement, an organization that sought to open up more opportunities for artists of color. The group staged protests on numerous TV shows (Ed Sullivan's, Johnny Carson's and a notorious 1970 incident on Dick Cavett's) in order to call attention to their cause.

As a barometer of the times, *Hard Luck Soul* (1972) was an album released by one of the state's most unusual jazz groups, the Ohio Penitentiary 511 Jazz Ensemble. Led by alto sax player Logan Rollins from Wheelersburg, the ragtag group of inmates performed his original compositions such as "Psych City" and "Mantra Dance" to the most captive of all audiences.

In 1969, Rusty Bryant♪ returned—and in a big way. Signed to Prestige Records, he cranked out a series of seven albums beginning with *Rusty Bryant Returns* (1969) and ending with *Until It's Time for You to Go* (1974) that are now regarded as soul jazz and/or acid jazz classics. As usual, he carried plenty of local talent with him, including Bill Mason (organ), Wilbert Longmire (guitar), Eddie Brookshire (bass) and Ernest Reed (guitar).

Cincinnati's Wilbert Longmire, putting aside thoughts of becoming a barber, got his start with Bryant and Hank Marr♪ before his friend George

Benson introduced him to Bob James. James was starting his own label, Tappan Zee, and signed Longmire as one of his first artists. Three albums followed, the third of which, *With All My Love* (1980), got some airplay for the instrumental "Hawkeye." He has also played with Jack McDuff and recorded two albums with Trudy Pitts and remains active in the Queen City music scene.

Bill Mason (1948–   ) grew up playing piano, organ, drums, sax, clarinet, flute, bass, guitar, cornet and piccolo in his father's Columbus church. In addition to working with Bryant, he traveled the country for nine years as musical director for evangelist Leroy Jenkins. After his excellent album *Getting' Off* (1972), he left jazz behind to concentrate on his spiritual side.

Bassist Eddie Brookshire (1941–   ) moved to Dayton with his parents in 1950. After being discharged from the army in 1965, he began playing with Piney Brown, the Coasters and the Drifters and then formed his own fusion group, the Casual Society, which recorded a couple albums with Rusty Bryant. After playing with the likes of Johnny Lytle, Little Jimmy Scott, Elvin Jones, Norris Turney, Bootie Wood, Snooky Young and Lowell Fulson, he formed the Eddie Brookshire Orchestra back in his hometown.

At fifteen, Ernest "Pepper" Reed (1955–1999) was already a guitar phenomenon in Columbus. He made his recording debut on Bryant's *Wild Fire* (1972) album the same year and then was signed to Motown subsidiary Whitfield Records as a member of the band Nytro. He soon became a popular session player.

Drummer/vocalist Emidio DeFelice, aka "Dee Felice" (–1991) and pianist Frank Vincent had begun jamming together in 1956 and spent 1969 touring and recording with the "Godfather of Soul," James Brown. This was during his so-called lounge funk period when he released covers of "Strangers in the Night" and "That's Life." Along the way, they picked up bassist Lee Tucker from the Modern Jazz Disciples to complete their trio. Joining them on the tour was vocalist Gwen Conley from Columbus, soon to become one of the featured singers on Bob Braun's *50-50 Club* television show.

After going on the road with Mel Tormé, Mark Murphy and Johnny Hartman, the Dee Felice Trio returned to Cincinnati and became Mixed Feelings, a band that was compared to the Fifth Dimension and Blood, Sweat and Tears. Their vocalist was a then unknown Randy Crawford, who would become famous for her hit recording with the Jazz Crusaders— "Street Life" (1979). In 1972, the band moved into the local Playboy Club. Joining it were guitarist Bugsy Brandenburg and vocalists Brenda Woodrum and Mary Ellen Tanner.

Then, in 1984, Felice opened the Dee Felice Café in Covington, Kentucky, just across the river from Cincinnati, to provide Tri-State residents with a taste of New Orleans–style food and jazz. Although he viewed it as a way of continuing to play his music, he gradually brought in all forms of jazz. Another veteran of the Modern Jazz Disciples, Roy McCurdy became drummer for the house band, which backed visiting artists. Felice assembled a seven-piece Dixieland-swing group, the Sleep Cat Band, which included Bill Gemmer (trombone), Lou Lausche (bass), Tom Cahall (piano), Ted des Plantes (vocals/piano), Frank Powers (clarinet), Carl Halen (cornet) and Wayne Yeager (piano).

Another musician with ties to James Brown is keyboardist David Matthews (1942–　). A graduate of the University of Cincinnati, he got his start performing in the local music scene before joining James Brown. Relocating to New York City, he took advantage of his connection to Brown in pursuing freelance opportunities. Among the performers he worked with were bandleader Buddy Rich, singers Mark Murphy and Bonnie Riatt and the Starland Vocal Band. By the mid-1970s, Matthews was staff arranger for the CTI (Creed Taylor Incorporated) label, whose roster of artists included George Benson, Bob James, Freddie Hubbard and Hubert Laws. He has scored many Hollywood films and launched his own little-known but critically acclaimed group, the Manhattan Jazz Quintet.

Born Charles J. Thornton Jr. in Ironton, drummer Butch Miles (1944–　) studied at West Virginia State College before joining the Count Basie Band (1975–1979). He then worked with Dave Brubeck and Tony Bennett during the next couple of years, while playing and singing on his own album, *Butch Miles Salutes Chick Webb* (1979). Miles is equally comfortable playing big band swing, traditional Dixieland or hot jazz.

Cincinnati's Fred Hersch (1953–　), a child performer on the kids' program *The Skipper Ryle Show*, relocated to New York City in 1977 at the age of twenty-one. It wasn't long before this uncompromising pianist made his presence known as a performer, composer and bandleader. In a career cut short by his battle with AIDS, Hersch recorded more than forty-five albums. *Vanity Fair* magazine proclaimed him "the most arrestingly innovative pianist in jazz over the last decade or so."

A self-taught pianist, Dayton's Roy Meriwether started his career in his father's church. Turning professional at eighteen, he received a jazz composition fellowship grant from the National Endowment for the Arts in 1973. Three years later, he moved to New York City, where he has been performing and composing ever since. Critic Arnold Shaw wrote that Meriwether is a "two-fisted pianist who in this day of right-handed wizards has the sound of a champion, with thunder in his left hand and lightning in his right."

The younger cousin of tenor sax player Buddy Tate, Steve Potts (1943–   ) is a Columbus-born jazz saxophonist. Having studied with Charles Lloyd and Eric Dolphy, he moved to Paris in 1970 and played in groups with saxophonist Steve Lacy for thirty years.

Chuck Rainey (1940–   ), a Youngstown bassist, appeared with the King Curtis Band in 1964 before becoming a well-known studio player. He performed at the Montreux Jazz Festival in 1971 with Eddie "Cleanhead" Vinson and then worked with Aretha Franklin and Quincy Jones. Following the release of his solo album in 1972, he recorded with Steely Dan on *Pretzel Logic*, *Katy Lied*, *AJA* and *Gaucho*. Rainy's work illustrates the crossover capacity of jazz as the root for contemporary musical styles.

Another King Curtis alumnus is saxophonist Eugene "Gene" Walker, who looked up to hometown heroes Hank Marr, Rusty Bryant and Raleigh "Ol' Boss" Randolph for inspiration. He was with Curtis in 1964 as the opening act for the Beatles American tour, after which he performed with Jimmy McGriff, Gene Ammons and Jackie Wilson, while appearing on albums with Chris Columbo, Johnny "Hammond" Smith and Byrdie Green.

Keyboardist/composer Dave Burrell (1940–   ) of Middletown attended Howard University, the University of Hawaii and the Berklee School of Music before moving to New York in 1966. He had formed the 360 Degree Musical Experience and co-composed the 1979 jazz opera *Windward Passage* with saxophonist David Murray.

Many artists also were politically and culturally active in the 1970s, reflecting the temper of the times. For example, Rusty Bryant founded a music workshop program for disadvantaged children through the Columbus Metropolitan Area Community Action Organization and also developed the "Rusty Bryant Nite Train Foundation," a prison outreach program, after learning that one of his former sidemen had been incarcerated.

The Dark Days of Disco (1974–79), with its reliance on drum machines, synthesizers and a rock steady four-on-the-floor rhythm, put many musicians out of work, regardless of genre. Gigs became fewer and farther between, competition for what remained was keen and, of course, the pay was poor. That jazz survived at all was due more to love than commerce. Everyone had to take a day job. But there was light at the end of the tunnel.

12
The Future of Jazz

Jazz, the ten-part, nineteen-hour documentary directed by Ken Burns, came in for heavy criticism when it was broadcast on PBS in 2001. There was some minor quibbling about his coverage of the origins and development of jazz up through hard bop, but many felt he really got bogged down somewhere in the 1960s. In fact, the last four decades were glossed over in a single episode.

"The stories from 1975 on are not finished, and there is no resolve," Burns acknowledged. "I could spend fifty hours on the last twenty-five years of jazz and still not do it justice." The same challenge confronts those attempting to write a history of jazz. The closer to the present, the harder it is to put the music and musicians in perspective.

Trumpeter Nicholas Payton plays what most people would call jazz, but he doesn't. "Jazz died in 1959," he wrote in "On Why Jazz Isn't Cool Anymore." He pointed out that Miles Davis's *Kind of Blue* is the bestselling jazz album of all time, and it was released in 1959 (the same year as Dave Brubeck's *Time Out*). "Jazz is haunted by its own hungry ghosts. Let it die."

"[N]obody's listening," Terry Teachout of the *Wall Street Journal* declared. A dozen years after Congress passed a joint resolution declaring jazz to be "a rare and valuable national treasure," a National Endowment for the Arts survey revealed that between 2002 and 2008, the audience for jazz had declined (28 percent among adults), aged (from a median age of twenty-nine to forty-six) and become more elite (resembling that for classical music, nonmusical plays and ballet).

Teachout, a jazz musician turned writer, blames the musicians for taking themselves too seriously—being artists instead of entertainers. Marc Myers of JazzWax.com put the blame squarely on "jazz's abandonment of dance music in the late 1940s." However, he also believes that it is only as high art that jazz can survive because "there simply are too many other forms of disposable music out there that are far better at cashing in on tastes and trends." Musician and educator Kurt Ellenberger observed that if you earn a degree in jazz, odds are you will wind up getting paid to teach, not to play—a dragon eating its own tail.

Since its inception, more than a couple dozen distinctive jazz styles have evolved. Ironically, what started out as dance music in the ragtime era seems to be kept alive in the dance clubs and discos, particularly in Britain and Europe. Although Payton may no longer play "the j word," there are still many who self-identify as jazz musicians. However, jazz is seldom taken straight but usually with a spoonful of sugar—pop, rock, rhythm and blues, hip-hop or bluegrass—to help it go down easier or to reach a new audience.

What started as a fantasy about a super group of some of the city's best jazz soloists became a reality in 1980 when the Jazz Dream Team (actually two teams) was assembled for the Greater Columbus Arts Festival by writer and musician Arnett Howard. On "defense" were Bobby Pierce (keyboards), Kevin Turner (guitar), Lee Savory (trumpet), Jeff DeAngelo (bass), Vince Andrews and Randy Mather (saxes), Vaughn Wiester (trombone), Billi Turner (drums), Steve Grier (percussion) and Mary McClendon (vocals). On "offense" were Bobby Alston (trumpet), Rusty Bryant[55] and Sonny McBroom (saxes), Gary Carney (trombone), Hank Marr (organ), Don Hales (guitar), Cornell Wiley (bass), Greg Pearson (drums) and Jeanette Williams (vocals). The Dream Team was a good snapshot of the veteran and up-and-coming jazz talent available in the Capital City.

In fact, 1980 may have been the turning point in Ohio jazz. Perhaps concern about the health of America's music spurred people to take action. During the decade, many jazz studies programs were introduced at institutions of higher learning. Many classical jazz groups were formed in communities throughout the state. More festivals started popping up.

The Listen for the Jazz Project, produced by the Columbus-based Arts Foundation of Olde Towne (AFOOT), is one example of the many small service organizations working across the state to preserve and present Ohio's Jazz Heritage. At such events as the annual Community Festival (ComFest) and the Hot Times Community Arts & Music Festival, older musicians perform with the younger ones, providing them with guidance, experience and a direct connection to the past.

The Northeast Ohio Jazz Society in Cleveland got its start in 1977 as the result of an article in *DownBeat* with the headline, "How to Start a Jazz Society." The Art Tatum Jazz Heritage Society in Toledo began in 1980 as the Toledo Jazz Society with the stated purpose to present, protect and promote jazz—America's unique art form. The Central Ohio Hot Jazz Society has much the same goal.

From a supply side, there are still a lot of good jazz musicians out there who deserve an audience, far too many to adequately cover in this small volume. And yet, some mention should be made of a few of them (at the risk of offending the many). Consider it an impressionistic portrait of the state of jazz—JazzOhio!

The Jazz Arts Group (JAG) of Columbus was the brainchild of trumpeter Ray Eubanks, a professor at Capital University and a working musician.[56] Founded in 1973, JAG was designed to be a big band using the best jazz musicians available. It was created as a nonprofit performing arts organization, a novel concept at the time. It was wildly successful from the beginning and, in 1978, settled into a long run at Battelle Hall.

After two European tours, the band changed its named to Columbus Jazz Orchestra in 1996, retaining Jazz Arts Group as the name of the "umbrella" organization. Two years later, the ensemble moved its base of operations to the restored Great Southern Theatre. When Eubanks retired in 2002, trumpeter Byron Stripling was hired as artistic director following a nationwide search.

Some of the best musical talent to be found in Ohio has passed through its ranks, to wit: Ray Eubanks, Wes Orr, Stan Gilliland, Bob Birkhimer, Jerry Kaye, Bob Everhart, Dean Congin, Chris McCormick, Ben Huntoon, Lee Savory, Jim Powell, Dwight Adams and Byron Stripling (+vocals) (trumpets); Sonny McBroom (+flute), Burdette Green, Jim Gallagher, Byron Rooker (+clarinet), Burdette Green, Rusty Bryant, Vince Andrews, Steve Genteline, Jim Carroll, Michael Cox, Dan Smith, Gene Walker, Howard Johnson (+tuba), Hal Melia (+clarinet), Chris Keith, Chad Eby, Pete Mills and Carl Sally (saxes); Ola Hanson (+violin), Vaughn Wiester, Tom Dale, Mark Greenwood, Glen Griffith, Gary Carney, Gary Twining, Pat Lewis, Jim Masters, Patrick Lewis and Linda Landis (trombones); Mary McClendon, Meg Murphy, Jeanette Williams, Michele Horsefield-Carney, Karen Massie, Tia Harris Roseboro, Dick Mackey, Dwight Lennox, Kelly Crum Delaveris and Lisa Clark (vocals); Jim Curlis, Bob Breithaupt, Tony Martucci and Steve Grier (drums/percussion); Al Berry, Doug Richeson and Chris Berg (basses); Derek DiCenzo, Tom Carroll, Tim Cummiskey and Colin Lazarski (guitars);

A highly sought-after arranger, Gary Carney was also an amazingly lyrical trombonist. *Bob Byler.*

and Bobby Pierce, Bobby Floyd, Hank Marr, Erik Augis, Richard Lopez, Tony Monaco, Dave Powers, Dan Rowan and Mark Flugge (keyboards).

The Blue Wisp was once a neighborhood bar in O'Bryonville, a suburb of Cincinnati. However, in 1977, owner Paul Wisby instituted a jazz policy in the hope that it would attract a mellower crowd. Four years later, John Van Ohlen and trumpeter Don Johnson decided to assemble a big band to perform on Wednesday nights. In no time at all, the club's reputation as the place to hear hard bop had spread from coast to coast.

Other band members have included: Steve Schmidt (piano), Michael Sharfe (bass), Lynn Seaton (bass), Mike Andres (lead alto sax/soprano sax), Larry Dickson (baritone sax), Joe Gaudio (tenor sax), Jim Sherrick (alto sax), Herb Aronoff (tenor sax), Kirk Shields (trombone), Jeff Owen (tenor trombone), Paul Piller (tenor trombone), Bill Gemmer (trombone), Clarence Pawn (tenor trombone), Gary Langhorst (bass trombone), Scott Acree (trombone), Al Nori (trumpet), Rick Savage (trumpet/flugelhorn), Kevin Moore (lead trumpet), Jerry Conrad (trumpet), Jeff Folkens (trumpet), Tim Hagans (trumpet/flugelhorn), Larry Wiseman (trumpet), Al Kiger (trumpet/

flugelhorn) and Phil DeGreg (piano). Rusty Bryant (tenor sax), Hank Marr (organ), Cal Collins (guitar), Bud Shank (sax) and Katie Lauer (vocals) have been among the many special guest artists.

When Wisby died in 1984, his wife, Marjean, took over the club. But four years later, she lost her lease and had to relocate the Blue Wisp to a new location in the basement of Garfield Place. Following her death in 2006, the club was sold and had to move again. Through it all, the Blue Wisp Big Band has continued to play on, anchored by the drumming of Stan Kenton–veteran Van Ohlen. In 1993, *Cincinnati Magazine* selected its "Be Bop Band Dream Team": John von Ohlen (drums), Morgy Craig (tenor sax), Steve Flora (bass), Al Nori (trumpet) and Steve Schmidt (piano). All regularly played at the Blue Wisp.

According to co-founder Gary Scott, the Cleveland Jazz Orchestra grew out of a preexisting band called the Northcoast Jazz Orchestra, which rehearsed at Lithuanian Hall. He and a friend decided to form a new group just to do concerts. Calling themselves the Cleveland Jazz Orchestra, they debuted on May 20, 1984, at Peabody's DownUnder. Within a year, they were presenting a subscription series out of the Cuyahoga Community College Metro Campus Auditorium.

In 1987, Roland Paolucci was hired as the director of the band and began assembling the best North Coast talent available, including his protégé, Jack Schantz, featured trumpet soloist. When Schantz succeeded Paolucci in 1993, he set his sights on putting the band "on the jazz map." He wanted the Cleveland Jazz Orchestra to be the band of choice for singers and jazz groups coming into Cleveland. For sixteen years, Schantz worked to increase the ensemble's popularity and reputation, stepping down in 2009. Sean Jones, tapped as interim artistic director, was featured on Nancy Wilson's Grammy-winning album, *Turned to Blue* (2007).

Among its members have been Sean Jones, Dave Banks, John English, Steve Enos, Dennis Reynolds, Jack Schantz, Lou Pisani, Gary Scott and Kent Englehardt (trumpets); Chris Anderson, Chas Baker, Scott Garlock, Paul Hungerford and Paul Ferguson (trombones); Theron Brown, Rock Whermann, Jackie Warren, Mark Gonder and Roland Paolucci (keyboards); Jerome Jennings, Jim Rupp and Nate Douds (bass); Dave Morgan (drums/percussion); Barbara Knight, Judi Silvano, Ki Allen, Evelyn Wright, Delores Parker Morgan, Debbie Gifford and Helen Welch (vocals); Johnny Cochran, Dick Ingersoll, John Klayman, George Shernit Howie Smith, Dave Sterner, Brad Wagner, Rich Shanklin, Tom Reed and Joe Lovano (saxes).

For sixteen or seventeen years, Vaughn Wiester (1945–   ) taught arranging and jazz history at Capital University. Around 1992, he put

Arranger and bandleader Vaughn Wiester conducting his Famous Jazz Orchestra at the former Columbus Music Hall. *LFTJ.*

together his twenty-one-piece Famous Jazz Orchestra to play Oley's Lounge at the Olentangy Inn in Columbus. Taking his inspiration from the Blue Wisp Big Band, his intent was to play "mainstream jazz." A veteran of the Woody Herman and Riley Norris Bands, Wiester put together a "book" that included his own charts, as well as those of Herman, Kenton, Basie and other arrangers he admires, including Dick Cone and Al Waslohn. Musicians come from all over Ohio to participate in Wiester's Monday night concerts ("Sight-readin', Baby!") at the Clintonville Woman's Club.

The Dayton Jazz Orchestra has been keeping things lively down in the Gem City since October 1993. The sixteen-piece modern and traditional big band had its start as a music-reading ensemble, pulling in some of the best musicians in the community. It is currently led by John Harner and assisted by Vaughn Wiester. The roster has included: Tim Pence, Hap Ashenfelter, Jeremiah True, Rick Johnston, Jeff Spurlock, Dan Nicora, Josh Atkin, Bill Burns and Les Whittington (saxes); Linda Landis, Noah Bellamy, John Hoff, Vaughn Wiester, Tom Billing, Todd Couch and Denny Seifried (trombones); Scott Belck, John Harner, Reg Richwine, Al Parr, Dick Fox, Mark Wilcox and Bill Dixon (trumpets); Lars Potteiger and Jeff Black (keyboards); Don

Compston and Vinnie Marshall (percussion/drums); Tom Pompei and Jim Leslie (basses); and Steve Shininger and Rick Evans (vocals).

Such repertory jazz ensembles, as they are sometimes called, are ensuring that big band jazz remains alive in Ohio in much the same way that symphony orchestras do for the classical repertoire. However, smaller groups also play an important role in ensuring that jazz not only survives but also thrives and grows. While the club scene waxes and wanes, many jazz musicians have proven to be quite enterprising in getting their music before the public, especially since the introduction of the Internet. A simple video on YouTube.com can garner several thousand "hits" and catapult an artist to overnight fame and, possibly, fortune.

Cincinnati's J Curve label was founded in 1999 to document the local jazz scene. Musicians performing on the initial release included: Jim Anderson (bass), Steve Barnes (drums), Bob Bodley (bass), Scott Burns (sax), Cal Collins (guitar), Phillip DeGreg (keyboards), Ron Enyard (drums), Paul Plummer (tenor sax), Ray Felder (alto sax), Brent Gallaher (tenor sax), Joe Gaudio (baritone sax), Brad Goode (trumpet), Art Gore (drums), Matt Green (piano), Jakubu Griffin (drums), Patrick Kelly (piano), Wilbert Longmire (guitar), Paul Patterson (violin), Jim Perkins (electric bass), Paul Piller (trombone), Kenny

Trombonist Sarah Morrow, the first female instrumentalist in the Ray Charles Orchestra, has established an international reputation. *Sarah Morrow.*

Poole (guitar), Steve Schmidt (piano), Bobby Scott (drums), Michael Sharfe (bass), Sandy Suskind (flute/sax), Frank Vincent (piano), Marc Wolfley (drums) and Wayne Yeager (piano).

As a snapshot of the Queen City jazz scene, this album could not be bettered and has helped to draw attention to some of the area's best talent.

In writing a history of jazz in Ohio, there are many ways to categorize or classify the state's jazz musicians. For example, there are those who share a Ray Charles connection:

- Columbus bassist Roger Hines (1952–　) played with Charles (1980–1987) before serving as musical director for vocalist Diane Schuur (1998–2004).
- Pickerington trombonist Sarah Morrow (1969–　), the first female instrumentalist to tour with Charles, has also performed with Dee Dee Bridgewater, David Murphy and the Duke Ellington Orchestra.
- Columbus tenor saxophonist Rudy Johnson (unknown–2007) was a disciple of John Coltrane who toured and recorded with Charles for thirty years and also played on Lamont Johnson and Bill Cosby's musical ventures.
- Columbus guitarist Kevin Turner toured with Charles and also worked with Hank Marr, Kim Pensyl and Gene Walker.

Or those (mostly Cincinnatians) who have worked with James Brown:

- Tenor sax player Jimmy McGary backed Brown on many King releases before going on to play with Miles Davis, Buddy Rich, Slide Hampton and Rahsaan Roland Kirk.
- One-time central Ohio resident J.C. Davis was the tenor sax–playing leader of the original Famous Flames.
- Drummer Dee Felice, pianist Frank Vincent, bassist Lee Tucker and other numerous session players at King Records (including funk bassist Bootsy Collins) played with Brown.
- Keyboardist David Matthews (1942–　) joined Brown in 1970 as an arranger and bandleader.

Some have charted new territory:

- Columbus's Joseph "Foley" McCreary Jr. was Miles Davis's "lead bass" player (1987–91) and has worked with a diverse group of artists, including George Clinton, Herbie Hancock, Macy Gray and David Sanborn.

- Considered one of the most avant-garde saxophonists on the scene, Cincinnati's Rick VanMatre is the leader of his own quartet, which incorporates art, drama, world music and aleatoric (i.e. based on chance) computer music into its performances.
- A major figure in New York's experimental music scene, Cleveland's Elliott Sharp (1951–) frequently performs on guitar, saxophone and bass clarinet and was among the earliest musicians to use a laptop computer in his performances.
- Jazz guitarist/composer James Emery (1951–) from Youngstown formed the String Trio of New York with Billy Bang and John Lindberg, in addition to working with Thurman Barker, Wadada Leo Smith and Henry Threadgill.
- Yellow Springs drummer Cindy Blackman (1959–), wife of guitarist Carlos Santana, has worked with Pharoah Sanders, Cassandra Wilson and Lenny Kravitz.

And some are winning plaudits from the critics:
- Rocky Ridge's Christian Howes (1972– ; "[T]here is nobody better than this guy," according to guitarist Les Paul) has played with Randy Brecker, Steve Turre and Spyro Gyra and was 2011 *DownBeat* Critics' Poll winner in the category of rising star/jazz violin.
- Columbus pianist Aaron Diehl, hailed by the *Chicago Tribune* as "the most promising discovery that [Wynton] Marsalis has made since Eric Reed," is the 2011 Cole Porter Fellow in Jazz of the American Pianists Association.
- At sixteen, Cincinnati pianist William Menefield became the youngest recipient of an *Applause* magazine Imagemaker Award; two years later, his debut album, *Big Will Leaps In*, reached number thirteen on the Gavin Jazz Charts.

Ohio musicians are apt to turn up anywhere:
- Pianist John Sheridan (1946–) from Columbus is best known for his twenty-two years with the Jim Cullum Jazz Band on the *Riverwalk, Live from the Landing* radio broadcasts, during which he contributed over one thousand arrangements.
- A Dayton-native, Grammy-nominated trumpeter Tim Hagans (1954–) worked in Europe with Dexter Gordon, Kenny Drew and Thad Jones and spent fourteen years in Sweden as artistic director/composer-in-residence for the Norrbotten Big Band.

- When Count Basie died in 1984, trombonist Mel Wanzo recommended Cleveland's Carl "Ace" Carter (1931–1996), a guy he had played with thirty years before, to replace him at the piano. Rather than trying to imitate Basie, Carter simply played the way he always had—Cleveland style—and it fit right in.
- During a sixty-year career as a drummer, Youngstown's Shedrick Hobbs traveled the country with Charlie Parker, "Big Joe" Turner, the Four Tops, the Temptations and Gladys Knight and the Pips. He taught many drummers, most notably Steve Gadd.

They have frequently worked as sidemen (and women) to some of the biggest names in the business:
- Pianist/composer Harold Danko (1947–) from Youngstown has played piano with the bands of Chet Baker, Woody Herman, Thad Jones/Mel Lewis, Gerry Mulligan and Lee Konitz.
- Columbus bassist Doug Richeson (1952–) worked with Tony Bennett for four years, recording three Grammy Award–winning albums, and also spent two summers with the Phil Collins Big Band.
- Guitarist Jeff Golub (1955–) from Akron is best known for supporting singer Rod Stewart on four albums and Billy Squier on seven.
- Cincinnati bassist Michael Moore (1945–) worked with Woody Herman, Marian McPartland, Freddie Hubbard, Benny Goodman, Chet Baker and Lee Konitz before joining the Dave Brubeck Quartet in 2008.

And not a few are out making it on their own:
- The son of a Cleveland legend, Eddie Baccus Jr. (1970–) is a member of the internationally known smooth jazz group Pieces of a Dream and has also worked with Atlantic Starr, Grover Washington Jr. and George Benson.
- Earl Neal Creque (1940–2000), longtime Cleveland resident, was a Grammy-nominated jazz composer from the Virgin Islands who worked as a session player with Stanley Turrentine, Grant Green, Bernard Purdie, Eddie "Cleanhead" Vinson and Teresa Brewer.
- Cleveland's John Fedchock (1957–), trombonist/bandleader/ arranger, worked with Gerry Mulligan, Louie Bellson and Rosemary Clooney, as well as his own New York Big Band.
- The seriously intense jazz guitarist Sandy Nassan (1947–) was signed to Herbie Mann's short-lived Embryo Records in 1970 and released one sterling album, *Just Guitar*.

However, many players have elected to stay home to perform to local audiences who might not always be as appreciative as they should be—audiences that don't realize that a musician can be both local and really good. Perhaps drummer Art Gore, who toured and recorded with guitarist George Benson before settling back in Cincinnati, put it best. "When I leave here, I'm famous," he noted. "I can go to Japan and Europe and people know who I am."

And the list goes on: musicians drawing their inspiration from jazz's rich past and taking it to the next level, wherever or whatever that might be. Experimental pianist Robert Glasper, who borrows liberally from jazz, R&B and hip-hop, refuses to get drawn into arguments over what to call his music: "You can't push harmony any further without it being free jazz—and that's old."

Jazz is dead only to those who try to define it out of existence. It is dead only to those who seek to put it in a box. It is dead only to those who feel they are the final authority on what is or isn't jazz. In response to Alexander Gelfand's article, "Life After the Death of Jazz," D.K. Dike commented: "[T]he heart of jazz is innovation and exploration and that anyone attempting to define jazz is asking to turn jazz into a fossil when it deserves to be alive, breathing and ever-changing. Clearly, the future of jazz doesn't include jazz police mumbling 'that's not jazz.'"

But whatever you call it, "If America has a future, jazz has a future," to quote theoretician/composer (and Ohio native) George Russell. "The two are inseparable." The Ohio Jazz Family Tree continues to grow, as more new artists from Ohio become part of the ongoing musical journey of jazz in America.

13

Sixty Brief Biographies

If you find yourself in Nelsonville and somebody mentions the "great Jackie Martin" (1916–1981), just play along. Chances are you've never heard of this big band–era saxophonist who first went out on the road during the 1930s while a student at Ohio University. His résumé included stints with Charlie Barnett, Kay Kyser, Meredith Willson and Ted Lewis before finishing his career with the Champagne Music Man himself, Lawrence Welk. While he may not have been in the same league as, say, Ben Webster or Jimmy Dorsey, there are some folks in his hometown who once believed a Jack Martin museum would be a major draw.

Museums have been built for other Ohio musicians, though. There is a very nice one in Circleville dedicated to Ted Lewis, once the highest-paid entertainers in the world. And even now it survives as a labor of love (make a point to visit it if you can).

In the following biographies, the authors profile sixty jazz musicians who called Ohio home.[57] They should be regarded as representative figures from Ohio's rich jazz history.[58]

CHARLIE ALEXANDER: DIPPER'S PIANO PLAYER (1904–1970)

Despite Louis Armstrong once jokingly introducing him as being from New Orleans, pianist Charlie Alexander actually called Cincinnati home. In his youth, he studied music and played saxophone and piano in local theater orchestras accompanying silent movies. Relocating to Chicago, Alexander

The Listen for the Jazz All-Star Band plays at Comfest Stage, *from left to right*: Arthur Baskerville, David Powers, Derek DiCenzo, Tom Carroll, Gene Walker, Paul Renfro, Reggie Jackson, Paul Cousar, Tony Jacobs and Lee Savory. *Kojo Kamau.*

briefly played the theater circuit with J. Rosamund Johnson before joining the bands of clarinetist Johnny Dodds and drummer Baby Dodds (1927–1929), as well as vocalist Lil Armstrong. These were all very traditional, New Orleans–style ensembles.

In the spring of 1931, Armstrong hired Alexander for his newly organized big band, and he stayed with it until the group broke up. On their hit recording of the old plantation song "When It's Sleepy Time Down South" (1931), Armstrong (whom Alexander calls "Dipper") and Alexander are heard bantering about going back down South, providing an ironic counterpoint to the song's racially insensitive lyrics. In fact, the band did tour the South, providing Armstrong with his first opportunity to revisit New Orleans since he became its most famous export. However, in contrast to Armstrong's Hot Fives and Hot Sevens, this was a "sweet" band, influenced by the sound of Guy Lombardo—Armstrong's favorite band! Alexander later worked in Chicago before finally settling in California.

ALBERT AYLER:
NAKED AGGRESSION IN JAZZ (1936–1970)

Music was a constant in the Ayler household in Cleveland: their father played the sax and the violin, brother Don played the trumpet and Albert played the alto sax. When he was ten, Ayler studied at the Academy of Music. His earliest musical influences were Lester Young, Sidney Bechet and Charlie Parker. He was even nicknamed "Little Bird" for his Parker-influenced style. After a stint in the Army Special Services Band, where he switched to the tenor sax, Ayler moved to Sweden and recorded *My Name Is Albert Ayler* (1966), considered one of the classics of the "new" music.

When Ayler returned to the United States, Attorney Bernard Stollman founded ESP-Disk specifically to record him. The label's first release was the groundbreaking *Spiritual Unity* (1964), quickly followed by *Bells* (1965), on which he was joined by his brother. Controversy raged about Ayler's primal sax sound, with some saying he couldn't play and others claiming that he was the "New Messiah of Jazz." Critic John Litweiler wrote that "never before or since has there been such naked aggression in jazz." His work is said to have influenced a young John Coltrane, who once claimed Ayler was his favorite musician (and requested that he play at his funeral).

MYRON "TINY" BRADSHAW:
THE TRAIN KEPT A' ROLLIN' (1905–1958)

Tiny Bradshaw left his home in Youngstown to major in psychology at Wilberforce College, where he sang with Horace Henderson's Collegians. A pianist as well as a drummer, he later worked with Marion Handy's Alabamans, the Savoy Bearcats and the Mills Blue Rhythm Band before joining Luis Russell as a vocalist. In 1934, Bradshaw left Russell to form his own swing group, which made its debut at the Renaissance Ballroom in New York and later that year recorded for Decca. Although he is often compared to his contemporary Cab Calloway, Gunther Schuller pointed out that he actually sang in a fairly advanced jazz style. And he never stopped swinging.

Gradually, however, Bradshaw left jazz behind during the 1940s and moved into rhythm and blues. His band achieved national fame with five charted songs on the King label, including "Train Kept A' Rollin'" (1951) and "Well, Oh Well" (1952). Although he continued to lead combos throughout

An autographed photo of Tiny
Bradshaw, swing musician and bestselling
rhythm and blues artist. *LFTJ.*

the 1950s, he suffered a couple of strokes that left him partially paralyzed. His final recording session took place in 1958, when he cut "Bushes" and "Short Shorts" in an effort to crack the teen market. However, a third stroke the same year ended his life.

Royal G. "Rusty" Bryant: All Nite Long (1930–1991)

Born in Huntington, West Virginia, Rusty Bryant grew up in Columbus, where he was a longtime fixture on the local jazz scene. The product of a musical family, he taught himself to play the sax and landed his first professional gig with pianist Archie "Stomp" Gordon within a week. He also went on the road with Tiny Grimes and His Rocking Highlanders before forming his own group in 1951. Booked into the Carolyn Club, he recorded a series of no-frills rhythm and blues 45s for the Dot label, including his biggest hit, "All Nite Long" (1954), a double-time version of "Nite Train." Soon, he was touring the United States in support of his recordings.

When his contract with Dot came to an end, Bryant returned home to work mostly in the Midwest, often with his former band mate Hank Marr. Then, in 1968, he backed organist Richard "Groove" Holmes on an album and was given the opportunity to lead his own recording sessions for Prestige

A promotional photo for Royal "Rusty" Bryant when he was being represented by the Gale Agency. *LFTJ.*

Records. Suddenly, he was hot again, turning out a series of seven albums from 1969 to 1974, starting with the highly regarded *Rusty Bryant Returns* and including the classic *Soul Liberation*. Bryant was a founder of Music in the Air, a free summer series.

GARVIN BUSHELL: SIDEMAN AND JAZZ HISTORIAN (1902–1991)

A native of Springfield, Garvin Bushell started piano at the age of six and clarinet at thirteen (later adding the flute, oboe and bassoon). Although never a star, he did play with many of the greats, and his memoirs of the jazz age are some of the best by an insider. Bushell studied at Wilberforce College before touring with Mamie Smith's Jazz Hounds (1919–20), Ethel Waters's Black Swan Jazz Masters under the direction of Fletcher Henderson (1921–22), Sam Wooding's Orchestra (1925–28), Fletcher Henderson's Orchestra (1935–36), Cab Calloway (1936–37) and Chick Webb (1937–39). Musically sophisticated and technically accomplished, Bushell could well have been a classical musician given the opportunity.

In 1941, Bushell formed his own sextet that performed through 1947. He joined the Chicago Civic Orchestra in 1950 and played in Fletcher Henderson's Reunion Band in 1958. For the next five years, he worked with Wilber DeParis before rejoining Cab Calloway in 1966. He spent the remainder of his life teaching music in Puerto Rico. In addition to Bessie Smith, Bushell recorded with Bunk Johnson, Cab Calloway, Chick Webb, Rex Stewart and Sam Wooding. On an early recording of "Sippi" (1928) by the Louisiana Sugar Babes, Bushell became the first artist to record a jazz oboe solo.

Multi-instrumentalist and jazz historian Garvin Bushell, whose career spanned 1916 to the 1980s, circa 1937. *DS.*

CHARLES WILLIAM "BILLY" BUTTERFIELD: THE BEST ALL-AROUND TRUMPET PLAYER (1917–1988)

Middletown's Billy Butterfield began playing music at the age of thirteen and didn't stop for the next fifty-eight years. He tried the violin, bass and trombone before settling on the trumpet. While studying medicine at Transylvania College in Kentucky, he played in campus bands before quitting school to join Austin Wylie in Pittsburgh, Pennsylvania. He soon moved on to Bob Crosby's Bobcats (1937–40). In the opinion of fellow band mate Max Herman, Butterfield was the best all-around trumpet player of the big band era.

As a member of the Artie Shaw band, Butterfield appeared in the movie *Second Chorus* (1940). The same year, he performed a "legendary" trumpet solo on the hit recording of "Stardust." Leaving Shaw a year later, he played with Benny Goodman and Les Brown before becoming a studio musician. From 1943 to 1945, Butterfield served in the army and then led his own

A publicity photo of Billy Butterfield, who quit medicine to become a full-time musician. *DS.*

band until 1947. During the late 1940s and 1950s, he worked as a session player and recorded two albums with Ray Coniff and a couple more with his own orchestra. In 1958, he performed at the Newport Jazz Festival with Benny Goodman. After spending 1968 to 1973 with the World's Greatest Jazz Band, he resumed his freelance musical activities.

ROBERT "BOBBY" BYRNE: THE KID WHO REPLACED TOMMY (1918–2006)

Born in Pleasant Corners, Bobby Byrne was the son of a noted music teacher. A child prodigy, he excelled on the trombone and harp but also played piano, piccolo, flute and cello. When Tommy Dorsey left the Dorsey Brothers Band, Jimmy Dorsey asked him to take his brother's place. He was only sixteen, but he was already starting to achieve his parents' dream for him. In 1939, Byrne left Jimmy Dorsey to form his own group. Byrne had good looks, natural ability, experience, a big band booking office that believed in him and a recording contract with Decca Records. Very quickly, he was getting the best jobs in the country.

The Jimmy Dorsey Orchestra meets Louis "Satchmo" Armstrong. The "kid" standing third from the right is Bobby Byrne, circa 1936. *DS.*

When World War II broke out, Byrne enlisted as a pilot. However, he soon was put in charge of the 618th Army Air Force Band. Following his discharge, he discovered the music business had changed, so he applied himself to becoming a top session player. Working with record executive Enoch Light, he arranged and produced many recordings for Grand Award and, later, Command Records. Although Roger Kinkle described him as an "excellent trombonist whose cool jazz solos in the 1930s were ahead of their time," Byrne denied ever having been a jazz musician.

Una Mae Carlisle: The Female Fats Waller (1915–1956)

The pride of Xenia (although family records indicate she was born in Zanesville), Una Mae Carlisle began singing publicly at the age of three and studied the piano throughout her childhood. By 1932, she had come

As beautiful as she was talented, Una Mae Carlisle (seen in 1938) had a meteoric career and died much too early. *DS.*

to the attention of her idol, Fats Waller, who booked her on his popular WLW radio show. For the next two years, Carlisle toured with Waller and recorded the duet "I Can't Give You Anything but Love" (1939). She closely emulated her mentor, playing piano in his boogie-woogie style and infusing her performances with humor. In 1939, Carlisle went to Europe with the *Blackbirds Revue*. Remaining in France, she headlined at her own club in Montmartre while studying harmony at the Sorbonne.

A year after returning to the United States, Una Mae became famous for two of her compositions, "Walkin' by the River" (1940) and "I See a Million People" (1941), recorded for Bluebird Records. Among her sidemen were such greats as Benny Carter, Lester Young and John Kirby. By 1952, Carlisle had written over five hundred tunes, was a popular nightclub performer and had her own radio show. However, rapidly declining health forced her to retire the same year.

TADLEY EWING PEAKE "TADD" DAMERON: THE ROMANTICIST OF THE BOP MOVEMENT (1917–1965)

Described by Dexter Gordon as "the romanticist of the bop movement," Tadd Dameron began his musical career learning saxophone from his brother, Caesar, in their Cleveland home. His first professional gig was in the mid-1930s as pianist with the Freddie Webster Band. He then joined the Zack Whyte and Blanche Calloway orchestras and began composing and arranging. After working in the Vido Musso Orchestra and Harlan Leonard Band (1939–41), Dameron contributed music and arrangements to the

The multitalented Tadd Dameron, photographed in New York City between 1946 and 1948. *WG-LOC.*

orchestras of Jimmie Lunceford, Billy Eckstine and Count Basie, including one of his best-known originals, "Good Bait."

Both Charlie Parker and Dizzy Gillespie recorded Dameron's "Hot House" in 1945. He also worked with Sarah Vaughn, Babs Gonzales and Fats Navarro. Two years later, *Esquire* honored him as the "Best New Jazz Arranger." In 1949, Dameron led an ensemble at the Royal Roost that included Miles Davis. In the same year, he co-led a quintet with Davis at the Paris Jazz Fair. Over the next few years, Dameron arranged for Artie Shaw, Pearl Bailey, Bull Moose Jackson, Carmen McRae, Max Roach, Sonny Stitt and Milt Jackson. The composer of "If You Could See Me Now" and many other beautiful ballads, Dameron stands at the crossroads between swing and bebop.

WILLIAM EDWARD "WILD BILL" DAVISON: THE TRUMPET KING (1906–1989)

Born in Defiance, "Wild Bill" Davison started out on the banjo, mandolin and guitar before switching to cornet and mellophone while in high school. Soon, he was playing in various local bands, including the Ohio Lucky Seven, James Jackson's Band and Roland Potter's Peerless Players. He made

"Wild Bill" Davison, the gunslinger of horn players, as he looked in 1950. *DS.*

his first recording in 1924 at the age of eighteen with the Chubb-Steinberg Orchestra. It was recorded in the back room of an appliance store. For most of the 1930s, Davison worked in Milwaukee, where he was billed as the "Trumpet King." To quote John S. Wilson, his was "the cockiest, sassiest, and even blowiest trumpet style in jazz."

However, Davison did not earn his nickname for his playing but rather his living. Until he stopped drinking cold turkey at the age of seventy-eight on doctor's orders, he admitted he had seldom played sober. Nevertheless, he was always in perfect control of his instrument. Davison worked in New York from 1941 to 1942 before joining the army. After the war, he hooked up with Eddie Condon and continued to play and tour both in America and Europe. In 1978, he performed at the Newport Jazz Festival. Over the course of his career, he appeared on hundreds of recordings.

WILLIAM "BUDDY" DE ARANGO: RECLUSIVE GENIUS OF THE GUITAR (1921–2005)

A native of Cleveland, self-taught guitarist Buddy De Arango played in Columbus-area Dixieland combos while attending Ohio State University prior to World War II. Following his discharge from the army in 1944, he relocated to New York City and made his debut sitting in with Don Byas. Ben Webster, Byas's rival, was so impressed by his playing that he hired him the same night.

Guitarist Buddy
De Arango, Terry
Gibbs and Harry Biss
performing at the Three
Deuces, New York City
(1947). *WG-LOC.*

A year later, De Arango left Webster to work with Charles Parker and Dizzy Gillespie backing vocalist Sarah Vaughn on a recording session.

De Arango was one of the prime movers in the bebop movement. His 1946 recordings with Gillespie—"A Night in Tunisia," "Ol' Man Bebop" and "Anthropology"—are considered jazz milestones. He also co-founded his own band with vibraphonist Terry Gibbs. From a musical standpoint, things could hardly have been better. However, in 1947, De Arango turned his back on the big time and returned home to Cleveland. He opened a record shop and continued to play local gigs, eventually hooking up with sax man Ernie Krivda. Over the years, he moved into free jazz and even psychedelic rock. But at the age of seventy-two, he reemerged with a comeback album, *Anything Went* (1993), which demonstrated that his improvisational gifts were still intact.

LOIS DEPPE:
THE HANDSOME HEARTBREAKER (1897–1963)

Lois (pronounced "Lewis") Deppe had a brilliant career. Born in Springfield, he was trained by the voice coach for the great tenor, Caruso, and appeared in many stage plays. In 1920, he was the first African American man to sing

A talented singer and bandleader with the suave looks of a matinee idol, Lois Deppe had the young women standing in the aisles. *LFTJ.*

a continuous program on the radio. By 1921, Deppe, who also played sax, was performing in Pittsburgh when he discovered a teenage piano wizard, Earl Hines. Together they organized a band that eventually grew to fifteen pieces. From 1922 to 1924, the band traveled under the name Lois Deppe's Plantation Orchestra and also recorded for Gennett as Lois Deppe's Serenaders.

After losing Hines to Carroll Dickerson, Deppe returned to the stage. In 1927, he was cast in the landmark musical *Showboat.* Other Broadway shows followed, including *Carmen Jones* (1944). However, he had to drop out after three weeks due to illness. Columbus poet and historian Anna Bishop remembered Deppe's performances at the Empress Theater: "[H]andsome heartbreaker Lois Deppe would hit the stage. He probably performed for about fifteen minutes finishing with the song 'Chloe.' Whoever was at the organ would play the notes (and we were all holding our breath) da, da, da, da, then handsome Mr. Deppe hit the high note that began the song…WE WENT CRAZY!"

VICTOR "VIC" DICKENSON: MR. NICE (1906–1984)

A "natural ear" player, Vic Dickenson from Xenia had little formal training. However, he was one of the most tasteful players to ever take up the trombone. As a young man, Dickenson was severely injured in a fall from a ladder while working with his father, a plasterer. Unable to perform manual labor, he decided to try his hand as a musician. Starting in 1921, he played with the Elite Syncopators and several local bands in Columbus. In the 1930s, he joined the territory bands of Speed Webb and Zack Whyte. Continuing into the 1940s, Dickenson worked with Blanche Calloway, Claude Hopkins, Benny Carter, Count Basie and Eddie Heywood.

During the 1950s, Dickenson moved freely between the Dixieland-revival groups and straight-ahead jazz combos. It has been said that he was, essentially, the leader of every band he played in because he was held in such high esteem by his band mates. In 1961 and 1962, Dickenson teamed up with Wild Bill Davison. In 1968–70, he co-led a quintet with trumpeter Bobby Hackett. One of the most loved players on the scene, Dickenson is remembered for his kindness, humor and humility—and the simplicity and beauty of his playing.

LAWRENCE "BEAU" DIXON:
A GRAND RHYTHMIC STYLE (1895–1970)

Lawrence "Beau" Dixon made his way north from Chillicothe to join Sammy Stewart's band in Columbus. He was purportedly inspired to become a musician by his father. An accomplished banjo, guitar and cello player, Dixon soon began to make a name for himself when the Stewart Orchestra settled in Chicago. He also was a member of a recording trio, Dixon's Jazz Maniacs. A year later, he left Stewart's orchestra to join the Dave Peyton theater band.

After stints with various other groups, Dixon joined the Earl Hines Orchestra (1931–37). Hines allowed him not only to demonstrate his remarkable skills as a performer but also to contribute his own arrangements. It was during this period that he made some of his best recordings. After leaving Hines, Dixon freelanced around Chicago. During the 1950s

A jazz pioneer on banjo, guitar and cello, Lawrence "Beau" Dixon went a long way from his Chillicothe home. *LFTJ.*

and early 1960s, he joined Franz Jackson's Original Jazz All Stars, where he displayed his "grand rhythmic style on banjo" (to quote Eugene Chadbourne). He also played with pianist Lil Armstrong (Louis Armstrong's second wife) and bass man George "Pops" Foster. However, after a career spanning four decades, Dixon was forced to retire in 1963 due to poor health.

HARRY "SWEETS" EDISON: SINATRA'S TRUMPET PLAYER (1915–1999)

Born in Columbus, Sweets Edison moved to Kentucky to live with an uncle at the age of five and soon learned to play the pump organ. At eleven, he was stricken with typhoid fever and began to use the trumpet as a way to strengthen his lungs and heart. His mother later claimed that "he went to bed and got up with that horn." Returning to Columbus at fourteen, Edison played with the Earl Hood Band on weekends and learned to read music. He also worked with Morrison's Grenadiers up in Cleveland.

In 1937, Edison joined the Count Basie Band, where he picked up

the nickname "Sweets" from saxophonist Lester Young. He quickly became an important soloist and arranger for the group and was featured in the film *Jammin' the Blues* (1944). Edison remained with the Basie Band until it temporarily broke up in 1950. From 1952 to 1958, he was in demand as a session player for Nelson Riddle, Lionel Newman and Benny Carter. He can be heard on recordings by Billie Holiday, Frank Sinatra and Ella Fitzgerald. Edison played many dates with Frank Sinatra (who said Sweets was his favorite trumpeter), before rejoining Count Basie. Edison's style is still one of the most individualized in jazz.

He wasn't called "Sweets" for nothing—the great Harry Edison, one of the best horns in the business. *LFTJ.*

118

FRANK BENJAMIN FOSTER: THE LIVING LEGACY (1928–2011)

A native of Cincinnati, Frank Foster played alto sax and clarinet as a youth, switching to the tenor sax in 1947. After studying at Wilberforce University, Foster played in Detroit with Snooky Young, Wardell Gray and Elvin Jones. Following service in the Korean War, he joined Count Basie's Orchestra as an arranger and reed player (1953–1964). Foster's compositions—"Shiny Stockings," "Down for the Count" and "Blues Backstage"—were an important factor in Basie's success during this period. Although Thelonious Monk, Miles Davis and others tried to hire him away, he preferred the security (and steady paychecks) of Basie's band.

As a freelance writer, Foster contributed to albums by Sarah Vaughn and Frank Sinatra. He also released several albums of his own, including the aptly

named *Fearless Frank Foster* (1965). From 1970 to 1972, he rejoined Elvin Jones and played in the Thad Jones/ Mel Lewis Orchestra. Upon Basie's death, Foster assumed leadership of the Count Basie Orchestra (1986–95). Among Foster's many notable works is "The Lake Placid Suite," commissioned for the 1980 Winter Olympics. Foster also led several groups on his own, including the Loud Minority, which had thirteen horns and a rhythm section. In addition to winning two Grammy Awards for "Deedles' Blues" (1987) and "Basie's Bag" (1988), Foster received the Living Legacy Award at the Kennedy Center.

A promotional piece featuring Frank Foster from the yearlong celebration All That Jazz at the Ohio Historical Society. *LFTJ.*

ARCHIE A. "STOMP" GORDON:
BELIEVE IT OR NOT (1926–1958)

"Two Tons of Torrid Fun," the always entertaining "Stomp" Gordon. *LFTJ*.

At the age of thirteen, Stomp Gordon was already something of a local celebrity in Columbus. His precocious talents as a singer and piano player were being displayed before such diverse audiences as the Nelsonville Eagles Club, Lafayette High School and Wilberforce University. The garage behind his Barthman Avenue home had become a magnet for other budding musicians (including a young Rusty Bryant). By the time he was sixteen, Gordon was working the Kiri Café, the Musical Bar, El Troviato and other clubs.

With his bright ties, dice shoe strings and zebra coat, Gordon was a wonder to behold, especially when he added more power to the bass by stomping on the piano keys with his bare feet! It was this feat that led to his being immortalized in a *Ripley's Believe It or Not!* newspaper cartoon. In his brief career, Stomp appeared on Ed Sullivan and in several movie shorts, accompanied Billie Holiday on an Alaskan tour and was ranked seventeenth-best pianist in the *DownBeat* poll and twenty-sixth in *Metronome*. He recorded a total of seventeen songs for four different labels. While some had predicted he would become the "next Fats Waller," his premature death cut short what had been a promising career.

JAMES CHARLES "J.C." HEARD:
THE DRIVER OF THE CAR (1917–1988)

Born in Dayton and reared in Detroit, drummer J.C. Heard worked with the bands of Bill Johnson, Sam Price, Milton Larkin and Teddy Wilson through the summer of 1942. Following a brief stint with Benny Carter, he joined Cab

Calloway (1942–45) and freelanced with Count Basie. In 1946, Heard led his own group at the Café Society in New York and performed in Norman Granz's Jazz at the Philharmonic shows. Returning to Count Basie's Orchestra in 1947, he began touring internationally.

Regarded as one of the most recorded and widely traveled drummers, Heard lived and worked in Japan from 1953 to 1957. Back in the United States, he again formed his own band and continued to freelance with groups

Drummer J.C. Heard takes a break from beating the skins (1951). ©*Herman Leonard Photography LLC.*

including the Coleman Hawkins' Quintet. After touring Europe with Sam Price (1958) and working with Teddy Wilson (1961), Heard led bands in Las Vegas and Detroit. During the 1970s and 1980s, his all-star band toured internationally. Dizzy Gillespie said that three men wrote the rules for modern jazz drumming: Kenny Clarke, Max Roach and J.C. Heard. "Everyone wants to play solos," Heard once told an interviewer, but who is going to keep the time? That's what the drum is. Basically, it is the driver of the car."

JOE A. HENDERSON: AN APTITUDE FOR MUSIC (1937–2001)

Tenor saxophonist and composer Joe Henderson came from Lima. Encouraged by his older brother, he studied music from 1956 to 1960 at Kentucky State College and Wayne State University, where his fellow students included Curtis Fuller, Donald Byrd and Yusef Lateef. Although he had already started composing and arranging before leaving home, Henderson's first true professional experience was in Detroit. He then worked briefly with Sonny Stitt and formed his own band in 1959 before

A promotional photo of the versatile Joe Henderson, who dedicated his first album to his parents and older brother for their support. *DS.*

touring the world with a U.S. Army band (1960–62).

Following his discharge, Henderson played with organist Jack McDuff and co-led a band with trumpeter Kenny Dorham but rose to fame in the bands of Horace Silver (1964–66) and Herbie Hancock (1969–70). His eclectic style combines bebop, rhythm and blues, Latin, avant-garde and soul. During the period from 1963 to 1968, Henderson performed on nearly thirty albums released on the Blue Note label. He later moved to California, where he freelanced as well as played in Freddie Hubbard's band, the Griffin Park Band, and the Echoes of an Era. Henderson was active as a teacher of his influential style of modern jazz. The winner of multiple *DownBeat* music awards, Henderson took home a Grammy for his album *So Near So Far: Musings for Miles* (1993).

JOHN CARL "JON" HENDRICKS: THE POET LAUREATE OF JAZZ (1921–   )

Jon Hendricks, an innovator of the singing style called vocalese, was called "the poet Laureate of Jazz" by critic and historian Leonard Feather. Born in Newark, he began singing as a child in church and at local banquets. When his family moved to Toledo in 1932, he began singing on the radio with family friend Art Tatum occasionally accompanying him. Hendricks spent a short time in Detroit, followed by service in the army (1942–46). Returning home, he studied at the University of Toledo and taught himself to play the drums.

In 1952, Hendricks moved to New York City and worked a series of jobs while continuing to compose. It was during this time that he wrote "I Want

A rare photo of (left to right) Dave Lambert, Annie Ross, Jon Hendricks, Sarah Vaughn and Helen Humes on stage together in 1959. *DS.*

You to Be My Baby." Five years later, he teamed up with Dave Lambert and Annie Ross to make multi-tape recordings in which each of them sang several parts to produce the effect of a full band. Hendricks wrote lyrics to Count Basie tunes, setting vocal notes to both the ensemble portions and the ad lib instrumental solos. The album *Sing a Song of Basie* (1958) was so successful that Lambert, Hendricks and Ross became a performing unit. He is a multiple Grammy Award winner and educator.

WALTER "PEE WEE" HUNT: THE HAPPY MAN OF DIXIELAND (1907–1979)

Pee Wee Hunt was born in Mount Healthy and grew up in Bexley. The product of a musical family (his mother played piano and banjo and his father violin), he started his professional career at age seventeen, playing banjo and teaching himself the trombone on the side. After high school, he attended Ohio State University and graduated from the Cincinnati College Conservatory of Music. Hunt worked with several Ohio bands, as well as the Paul Whiteman Orchestra. He was heard by the legendary Bix Beiderbecke, who recommended him for the Jean Goldkette Orchestra, which included Glen Gray on alto sax.

Walter "Pee Wee" Hunt upped the fun quotient when he tackled the old chestnut "Twelfth Street Rag" and made it a hit. *LFTJ.*

In 1929, Hunt and Gray came up with a plan for the Casa Loma Orchestra, a "co-op" band in which all musicians were shareholders. This group set the stage for the emergence of swing bands and the big band era. In 1943, Hunt left the group to become a disc jockey but soon joined the Merchant Marines. Five years later, while working with studio musicians, Hunt struck gold; his recording of "Twelfth Street Rag" sold more than three million copies. During the chorus, he would work the slide of his trombone with his foot. "It's hard on me," Hunt would announce, "but a lot rougher on you."

BENJAMIN CLARENCE "BULL MOOSE" JACKSON: BIG TEN INCH RECORD (1919–1989)

A blues and rhythm and blues singer and saxophonist, Bull Moose Jackson was a popular performer during the late 1940s. Born in Cleveland, he formed his first band, the Harlem Hotshots, while still in high school. In 1943, he landed a job with Lucky Millinder and was promptly nicknamed "Bull Moose." When singer Wynonie Harris was unable to perform at a show in Texas, Jackson was tapped to replace him. With Millinder's encouragement, Jackson soon signed a contract with King Records as an R&B artist. He had an immediate hit with "I Know Who Threw the Whiskey" (1946), an answer song to Millinder's "Who Threw the Whiskey in the Well."

Backed by the Buffalo Bearcats, Jackson racked up several more hits during the decade. Although he performed in a number of styles, he is best known for his bawdy jump blues songs. In 1951, his band included Tadd Dameron on piano and Benny Golson, serious jazz musicians who also crossed over to rhythm and blues because they enjoyed it and it paid the bills. In spite of his image, Jackson was a competent swing jazz player. Instead, his biggest hit was the not-suitable-for-airplay "Big Ten-Inch Record" (1952), recorded with the Tiny Bradshaw Orchestra.

Isham Jones:
Songwriter Extraordinaire (1894–1956)

Originally from Coalton, Isham Jones seemed destined to follow his father into the mines. However, after nearly being run down by a coal train, he quit the mines to focus on a career in music. In 1915, Jones moved to Chicago, where he led a trio and composed music, often with lyricist Olaf "Ole" Olsen. Their 1917 collaboration, "That's Jaz!" was one of the first songs to refer to the new musical style. Meanwhile, the Isham Jones Orchestra was steadily building a reputation as one of the best in the business. Although Jones played sax and piano, he never featured himself.

Jones was such a prolific composer that he actually wrote "Spain," "The One I Love Belongs to Somebody Else" and "It Had to Be You" during one evening in 1924. Many of his melodies have become part of the Great

Isham Jones was one of the first bandleaders to fuse jazz with swing. *Library of Congress.*

American Songbook. When jazz great Woody Herman went to work for Jones, he said it was the "big league." In 1936, Jones retired and turned his band over to Herman. Thereafter, he devoted his time primarily to composing and managing his Colorado ranch. Gordon Jenkins wrote that the Isham Jones Orchestra was "the greatest sweet ensemble of that time or any other time."

SAMMY KAYE: MR. SWING AND SWAY (1910–1987)

Born Samuel Zarnocay Jr. in Lakewood, Sammy Kaye attended Rocky River High School in Cleveland, where he played football, basketball and ran on the track team while studying clarinet and banjo. He also took up the saxophone but never distinguished himself on any instrument. As a student at Ohio University, he continued his athletic and musical pursuits. Kaye operated the Varsity Inn in Athens, led a collegiate orchestra and played in the school marching band. Somehow, he also managed to earn a degree in civil engineering.

After graduation, Kaye went on tour with Morey Brennan's Jazz Clowns before organizing his own group in 1933. By the mid-1940s, he had one

What's wrong with Sammy Kaye? Nothing at all, according to his millions of fans. *LFTJ.*

of the most popular bands going. His tagline was "Swing and Sway with Sammy Kaye." Part of his success was due to his gimmicks. So You Want to Lead a Band gave contestants an opportunity to lead the band, with winners decided by audience applause. *Sunday Serenade Book of Poems*, a radio program, consisted of reading poems while popular music played in the background. Kaye's biggest hit was his recording of "Daddy" (1941).

CARL "BATTLE-AXE" KENNY: THE WORLD'S GREATEST DRUMMER (1891–1969)

Battle-Axe Kenny's childhood home stood at 15 North Front Street, the current site of Columbus City Hall. He developed an interest in drumming at an early age and began his professional career with Parker's Popular Players. In 1912 or 1913, James Reese Europe's band came to Columbus with Vernon Castle's traveling show, *Watch Your Step*. When told of Kenny's talents, Europe challenged him to a battle with the band's regular drummer. The event took place at the Southern Hotel, and it was said that "Battle-Axe" was definitely the better of the two.

In 1916, Europe invited Kenny to join his group, the 369th Infantry Hell Fighters Band. Relocating to New York City, he soon competed for the title of the "World's Greatest Drummer." Kenny, who could play drums rolls with his foot on the bass drum, tied for first place with the drummer from the show *Castles in the Air*, and both were awarded gold medals. Kenny purportedly wore his medal every time he went out for the rest of his life. After Europe's death, Kenny played in the Broadway shows *Chocolate Dandies*, *Runnin' Wild* and *Blackbirds* before returning home. Years later, Paul Whiteman chose Kenny to be the percussionist in his all-star fantasy orchestra.

RONALD T. "RAHSAAN ROLAND" KIRK: THIS IS NOT A SIDESHOW (1936–1977)

Born in Columbus, Rahsaan Roland Kirk lost his sight at an early age. By age two, he was already trying to coax music out of everything, including a piece of garden hose. His mother taught him how to play the bugle, and at nine he learned the trumpet but gave it up when a doctor said the pressure of playing would put a strain on his eyes. Instead, he switched to the saxophone and clarinet. When Kirk was sixteen, he had a dream of playing

The one-man horn section, Rahsaan Roland Kirk, demonstrating "circular breathing." *LFTJ.*

three instruments at once. At a local music store, he found the instrument he was looking for in a box of odds and ends—a "Moon Zeller" (or manzello).

Kirk played with many jazz greats, but few could keep up with him when he played two or three instruments simultaneously. Accused of being a circus act, he would sometimes tell the audience before he began, "This is not a sideshow." Politically outspoken and a proponent of "Black Classical Music," Kirk was the leader of the Jazz and People's Movement. When he was paralyzed on one side by a stroke in 1975, he taught himself to play one-handed and resumed touring the following year. Among his many compositions was "Bright Moments" (1970).

ERNIE KRIVDA:
AN UNDERRATED COLOSSUS (1945–   )

Born Krvda Ernö in Cleveland, tenor saxophonist Ernie Krivda got his starting playing locally with bebop organist Eddie Baccus Sr. and guitarist Bill DeArango. As leader of the house swing band at the Smiling Dog Saloon, Krivda shared the stage with Chick Corea, Elvin Jones, Herbie Hancock and other jazz greats. He then went on tour and recorded with producer and arranger Quincy Jones, who heard about him from Cannonball Adderley. Relocating to New York City, he was promptly signed by Inner City Records for a series of acclaimed albums. Others have followed on the Cadence, Koch and Creative Improvised Music Projects labels.

After performing at the Kool and North Sea Jazz Festivals and Carnegie Hall, Krivda returned to his hometown in the 1990s and founded the Fat

Tuesday Band; he also became artistic director of the Cuyahoga Community College Jazz Studies Program. "It might be better for my career to live somewhere else," he said, "but it's better for my art to live in Cleveland." A touring clinician for the Yamaha Instrument Company, Krivda continues to perform throughout the country, particularly "the circuit" (Pittsburgh, Detroit, Chicago, Indianapolis, Columbus and Cincinnati). W. Kim Heron, writing in the *Detroit MetroTimes*, said Krivda is "an underrated colossus."

TED LEWIS:
THE HIGH-HATTED TRAGEDIAN OF SONG (1890–1971)

Obsessed with music from his earliest years, Circleville's Ted Lewis (born Theodore Leopold Friedman) learned to play clarinet in the traditional klezmer style. His family did not share his enthusiasm for music, however, and tried to steer him toward a career in business. Instead, Lewis went into vaudeville around 1906. While working his way to New York with a comedian named Eddie Lewis, Ted was erroneously billed on a marquee as Lewis instead of Friedman. Soon, the name Ted Lewis would be world famous.

In 1917, Lewis won his trademark battered top hat from a hansom cab driver in a game of chance. The hat became a part of his persona, as did

Ted Lewis was hailed as the "Jazz King" in the early days of the dance band era. *DS.*

his catch phrase: "Is Everybody Happy?" Mark Berresford noted, "Lewis whistles, sings, toots a cruel clarinet and plays a melodious sax…but chiefly Lewis is a *poseur*, a strutter, a jazz hound, and a showman." And by 1925, he was the highest-paid man in show business. He was also a first-rate judge of talent whose band included a who's who of future jazz stars. During a career that spanned half a century, Lewis made hundreds of recordings, many of which were major hits. His recording of "Tiger Rag" (1925) sold five and a half million copies alone!

JOSEPH SALVATORE "JOE" LOVANO: BIG T'S SON (1952–   )

Inspired by his father, tenor saxophonist Tony "Big T" Lovano, Joe Lovano started on alto at age six and tenor five years later. Two of his brothers also played sax, while a third played trumpet. By the time he was sixteen, he was a professional musician, sometimes subbing for his father. After high school, he enrolled at Boston's Berklee College of Music. Gigs as a sideman for organists Lonnie Smith and Brother Jack McDuff followed by a three-year tour with Woody Herman (1976–79) led to his joining the Mel Lewis Orchestra (1980–92).

In 1981, Lovano joined the Paul Motian band. Since then, he has worked with John Scofield, Herbie Hancock, Elvin Jones, Charlie Haden, Lee Konitz, Carla Bley, McCoy Tyner, Ornette Coleman and a host of others. Signed by Blue Note records, he has scored eight Grammy nominations and a win for the album *52ⁿᵈ Street Themes* (2000).

The *New York Times* has heralded Lovano as "one of the greatest jazz musicians in history." In the *DownBeat* Critic Polls, he has won album of the year for *Bird Songs* (2011) and best jazz group of the year for *Us Five* (2010), as well as best jazz artist and tenor saxophonist of the year (both 2010).

JOHN DILLARD "JOHNNY" LYTLE: THE GREATEST VIBES PLAYER IN THE WORLD (1932–1995)

In Johnny Lytle's hometown of Springfield, a street was named in his honor—Johnny Lytle Avenue. Beginning in 1950, he drummed behind Ray Charles, Jimmy Witherspoon and Gene Ammons. As a youth, he had been given a vibraphone mallet by Lionel Hampton. However, it was not until the

A candid photograph of the sensational Johnny Lytle in concert. *LFTJ.*

mid-1950s that he began playing the instrument in earnest. Hampton would later proclaim Lytle "the greatest vibes player in the world." In 1957, he formed his own group and toured steadily in the United States and England. Signed to the Jazzville label three years later, he eventually released more than thirty albums on minor labels that showcased his remarkable talents as a vibes player and composer.

A dazzling musician and showman, Lytle is best known for such jazz classics as "The Village Caller" (1963), as well as "The Loop" (1964), "Moonchild" (1991) and "Selim" (1966). Throughout his life, he continued to be a popular, though not always well-paid, performer. He once played Redd Foxx's club in Los Angeles and accepted five of Foxx's suits as payment. Over the years, Lytle received numerous awards for his work as director of Springfield's Davey Moore Arts Cultural Center. Fittingly, his last performance was with the Springfield Symphony Orchestra.

ENRICO NICOLA "HENRY" MANCINI: COMPOSER TO THE STARS (1924–1997)

During his stellar career, Cleveland's Henry Mancini recorded more than ninety albums and won twenty Grammys, four Academy Awards and a Golden Globe. While he was justly famed for the many television and movie soundtracks

Our man Hank in Hollywood, Henry Mancini, one of the best-known and best-loved musicians of his generation. *LFTJ.*

he composed, as well as his numerous concert performances, what is less appreciated is his enormous impact on the popularization of jazz. He initially made his name with his jazz-infused scores for the TV shows *Peter Gunn* and *Mr. Lucky*, which inspired a generation of young musicians to take up playing jazz.

Mancini started on the piccolo at the age of eight and later played piano with local Pittsburgh bands while attending Carnegie Tech Music School. Later, he also went to Julliard. After military service, he played with Tex Beneke before moving to the West Coast, where he worked with Universal Pictures as a staff composer (1951–1957). By 1961, Mancini was thoroughly established as a composer for television and films. In 1964, '65 and '66, he was voted leader of the mythical All-Star Band in the annual *Playboy* Jazz Poll. Albums of Mancini creations have been recorded by virtually every artist of the 1960s through the 1980s, including jazz greats such as Sarah Vaughn and Quincy Jones.

HENRY "HANK" MARR:
THE PROFESSOR OF THE JAZZ ORGAN (1927–2004)

Hank Marr was born in the "Flytown" area of Columbus. As a boy, he would sneak off to play "boogie-woogie" on a neighbor's piano. Eventually, his father bought him one of his own. He also jammed with his friend

Ronnie Kirk. Although he developed a good ear, his musical education began when he replaced "R.C." (Ray Charles) in a Florida band, Charley Brantley and the Honey Dippers. Returning home, he entered Ohio State University on the GI Bill while performing with Sammy Hopkins and Rusty Bryant. The musical partnership between Bryant and Marr continued for forty years.

Inspired by Jimmy Smith, Marr took up the Hammond B-3 organ and formed his own trio in the mid-1950s. At the urging of his agent, he developed a more orchestral sound than that of his hero. In 1961, King Records signed him as

Hank Marr at the piano in Tampa, Florida, in the late 1940s. *LFTJ.*

a replacement for Bill Doggett. From 1968 to 1978, Marr worked as musical director for comedian George Kirby, traveling from coast to coast. Afterward, he returned to Ohio State as an associate professor in jazz studies. For more than two decades, Marr was the official keyboard player for the Columbus Jazz Orchestra. On August 12, 1990, the City of Columbus honored him with "Marvelous Hank Marr Day."

GENE MAYL:
THE DIXIELAND RHYTHM KING (1928–)

In 1946, tuba and string bass player Gene Mayl organized the first incarnation of the Dixieland Rhythm Kings in his hometown of Dayton, inspired by the original New Orleans "hot" jazz groups. "We just want people to hear a happy, rocking band that plays what we think is New Orleans jazz," he

The Dixieland Rhythm Kings, with Gene Mayl (bass) and Carl Halen (cornet), performing in Hamilton, Ohio. *DS.*

explained. He then took off to Paris for a couple years, where he played with Claude Luter, Don Byas and Claude Bolling. When he returned home, Mayl put the band together again. However, most of the original members gravitated to Carl Halen's Gin Bottle Seven.

In addition to his own group, Mayl worked with many traditional jazz all-stars, among them Muggsy Spanier, Billy Maxted, Wild Bill Davison and George Brunies. For many years he was a major force in the Dixieland movement of the Midwest. Mayl and his hard-swinging Dixieland Rhythm Kings made numerous recordings for Jazz Disc, Knickerbocker, Jazztone, Riverside (1953 and 1958), Audiophile, Jazzology, Blackbird, Red Onion and Fat Cat's Jazz. His best-known sidemen were cornetist Carl Halen, trombonist Bob Mielke, clarinetist Joe Darensbourg, trombonist Bootie Wood, cornetist Ernie Carson, pianist John Ulrich and singer Claire Austin. Mayl continued to be a popular performer on the jazz festival circuit.

THE MILLS BROTHERS—FOUR BOYS AND A GUITAR: JOHN SR. (1882–1967), JOHN JR. (1911–1936), HERBERT (1912–1989), HARRY (1913–1982) AND DONALD (1915–1999)

The four Mills Brothers of Piqua started off singing in the choirs of the local AME and Baptist churches. Before long, they were also performing in local vaudeville and tent shows and, in the late 1920s, were featured on radio station WLW in Cincinnati. The quartet was one of the first vocal groups to achieve great commercial success and was among the earliest African American ensembles to gather a national following. By 1930, they were in New York, performing, appearing in films and recording for the Brunswick label. When they co-starred on CBS radio's *Fleischmann's Yeast Hour* (1930–31) with Rudy Vallee, they were such an enormous hit that they soon had their own show, *Four Boys and a Guitar* (1932–33).

The Mills Brothers—Herbert, Harry and Donald—were discovered by a whole new audience in the 1950s. *LFTJ.*

John Mills Jr., who played guitar and sang bass in the group, died of pneumonia in 1936, leading John Mills Sr. to step into his son's shoes. The group continued its success with many hit songs, the best known being "Paper Doll" (1943), which sold six million copies. When Harry was drafted into the army during World War II, a non-family member, Gene Smith, was pressed into service until he returned a year later. They continued to be a popular act into the early years of rock-and-roll, scoring hits with "Glow Worm" (1952), "Opus One" (1955) and a handful of others. John Sr. retired in 1957 at the age of sixty-eight, but Herbert, Harry and Donald continued to perform as a trio throughout the 1970s. Over the course of their career, the Mills Brothers made more than two thousand recordings, sold more than fifty million records and earned at least three dozen gold records.

JAMES "JIMMY" MUNDY: LIVIN' THE LIFE (1907–1983)

Jimmy Mundy started on violin at age six in his hometown of Cincinnati. Although he could play many instruments, he focused mainly on the tenor sax. Leaving home, he played first with the Sammy Stewart Orchestra in

Three legends from the Count Basie band, *from left to right:* Jimmy Mundy, Lester Young and Walter Page. *DS.*

Columbus and Chicago (1926–29) and then with Erskine Tate, Carroll Dickerson and Earl Hines (1929–36). He also began developing his considerable arranging skills. Beginning in 1935, Mundy became the staff arranger for Benny Goodman and produced such works as "Swingtime in the Rockies" and "Solo Flight." Mundy subsequently produced arrangements for Gene Krupa (1938–39), Count Basie (1940–47) and Dizzy Gillespie (1949). He had tried his hand at leading his own band in 1939 but gave it up during World War II.

After leaving the military, Mundy resumed his career as an arranger for many of the biggest names in the business. He also wrote the score for the 1955 Broadway musical *The Vamp*, starring Carol Channing. Two years later, another musical, *Livin' the Life*, also included some of his work. In 1959, Mundy moved to Paris, where he became the musical director for Barclay Disques, a record company, before returning to New York. Although he sometimes played sax, it is for his brilliant arrangements, such as "Sing, Sing, Sing" for Benny Goodman, that Mundy is remembered.

JOSEPH PAUL "JOE" MURANYI: FROM LOUIS TO LAWRENCE (1928–)

Originally from Martins Ferry, Joe Muranyi was a jazz clarinetist who doubled on the ukulele and soprano sax and sometimes sang. His first professional job was playing with a symphonic balalaika orchestra. Although he studied with Lennie Tristano, he remained firmly rooted in early jazz styles. During World War II, Muranyi was a member of the U.S. Army Air Force Band. Following his discharge, he attended the Manhattan School of Music and Columbia University. In the 1950s, he played with Eddie Condon, Danny Barker and the Red Onion Jazz Band. Known for his wit,

Muranyi also was a producer and writer of liner notes for such major labels as Atlantic and RCA.

In 1963, Muranyi was a member of the Village Stompers, a Dixieland group that scored a major hit with "Washington Square" (number two on the *Billboard* pop charts) and released six albums. In 1967, he joined Louis Armstrong's All-Stars (Armstrong called him "Joe Ma Rainey"). Upon Armstrong's death, Joe went to play with Roy Eldridge. In 1975, he joined the World's Greatest Jazz Band and eight years later played with the Classic Jazz Quartet. Joe continued to tour as a soloist with Keith Smith and appeared in two TV documentaries about Louis Armstrong.

Joe Muranyi played with everyone from Louis Armstrong to Lawrence Welk and scored a hit with his recording of "Washington Square." *LFTJ.*

MELVIN JAMES "SY" OLIVER: CREATOR OF THE LUNCEFORD SOUND (1910–1988)

Although Sy Oliver was Michigan born, he grew up in Zanesville, where he started the trumpet at the age of ten and ran around with saxophonist Al Sears. During Oliver's sophomore year of high school, his father fell ill, so the teenager began playing professionally to help out his family. In 1927, he joined the territory band of Zack Whyte, remaining through 1930. Soon, he also began to compose and arrange music as well.

Oliver left Whyte's band and moved to Columbus, where he played in clubs around Ohio State University and tutored students. Crossing paths with Alphonso Trent, he was hired to write a new "book" (group of musical arrangements) to replace music that had been lost in a fire. In 1933, Oliver joined Jimmie Lunceford's Orchestra, which he described as "the first band to play for everybody." His arrangements, some of which he had carried over from his Zack Whyte days, established the Lunceford sound. From 1934

Sy Oliver, seen in 1946, wrote arrangements for everyone from Zack Whyte to Tommy Dorsey over the course of his celebrated career. *WG-LOC.*

to 1939, he wrote and sang for Tommy Dorsey's Orchestra. Just after the war, he formed his own band. Oliver continued to perform and arrange throughout the next couple of decades. In 1968–69, he directed a band in Paris, continuing to play well into the 1980s.

Donald "Don" Patterson: Sonny Stitt's Favorite Organist (1936–1988)

Originally inspired by Carmen Cavallaro, Don Patterson started learning piano while attending University High School in Columbus but later switched to organ when Hank Marr gave him his first opportunity to play the Hammond B-3 in 1959 at the Club Regal. As Marr later recalled, he "saw something in his eye…he was affected just like I was and decided he, too, had to play this thing." Largely self-taught, Patterson became a highly regarded bebop player who retained a distinctive "piano approach" to the instrument in contrast to Jimmy Smith's more fluid style and Marr's orchestral sound.

A Hammond B3 legend,
Don Patterson left behind
a significant body of
recorded works, which has
influenced legions of organ
players. *LFTJ.*

Patterson rose in combos and on recordings with the likes of Sonny Stitt, Eddie "Lockjaw" Davis, Gene Ammons and Booker Ervin. He also led his own group, frequently with drummer Bill James and guitarist Pat Martino, in a series of more than twenty albums. His musical interplay with such sax giants has been called "manic." Although commercial success eluded him (his bestselling album, 1964's *Holiday Soul*, took three years to reach number eighty-five on the *Billboard* chart), he is a legend among jazz organists.

KIM PENSYL: FROM JAZZ-POP TO NEW AGE (1954–   )

A prolific composer and arranger, Columbus-born keyboardist and trumpeter Kim Pensyl attended Ohio State University, where he was a member of the famed Jazz Ensemble, and the University of California, Northridge. He has performed with jazz legends Toots Thielemans, Al Hirt, Don Ellis, Hubert Laws and Gerald Wilson, as well as modern greats Joey Calderazzo, Bob Mintzer, Chiele Minucci, Andy Narell, Will Kennedy, Steve Rodby and Alex Acuna. Although he made his name as a keyboard wiz, he also can cut loose on the trumpet when he chooses to.

Twice named a *Billboard* Top 20 Contemporary Jazz Artist of the Year, Pensyl is on the jazz studies faculty at the College-Conservatory of Music in Cincinnati, where he has shared the stage with Arturo Sandoval, Terri Lyne Carrington and Mulgrew Miller. In addition to touring with the Woody Herman Orchestra and Acoustic Alchemy, he has appeared at the Clearwater Jazz Festival, Sunfest, Summerfest, Stone Mountain Jazz Festival and Pacific Jazz Festival. In 1989, ASCAP (American Society of Composers, Authors and Publishers) named him the "Best New Jazz Writer," while two years later NARM (National Association of Recording Merchandisers) chose *Pensyl Sketches #3* as the Jazz Album of the Year. Four of his albums reached the top ten on *Billboard*'s Contemporary Jazz chart.

KEN PEPLOWSKI: THE MAN IS MAGIC (1959–   )

Clarinetist and saxophonist Ken Peplowski has frequently been compared to Benny Goodman in terms of tone and virtuosity. Born in Cleveland, he first began playing in a Polish polka band. By the time he reached high school, he was teaching at a local music store. Peplowski left college after a year to join the Tommy Dorsey Orchestra (directed by Buddy Morrow) as lead alto sax player. In 1980, he moved to New York City, where he played everything from Dixieland to avant-garde jazz. Four years later, Benny Goodman came out of retirement and hired Peplowski to play tenor sax in his new band.

Soon, Peplowski was signed to Concord Records, for which he recorded nearly twenty albums as a leader. He has also collaborated with Mel Tormé, Charlie Byrd, Peggy Lee, George Shearing, Hank Jones, James Moody, Houston Person and Leon Redbone. It was Tormé who said, "Since the advent of Benny Goodman, there have been too few clarinetists to fill the void that Goodman left. Ken Peplowski is most certainly one of those few. The man is magic." In 2007, he was named jazz advisor of the Oregon Festival of American Music and music director of Jazz Party at the Shedd, both in Eugene, Oregon.

ARTHUR STERLING "ART" RYERSON JR.: THE GUITARIST'S GUITARIST (1913–2004)

At fourteen, Art Ryerson learned banjo from a door-to-door salesman in Columbus, soon switching to guitar. In the early 1930s, he joined the Rhythm Jesters at WLW radio in Cincinnati. Two years later, he moved to New York City and landed a gig at Nick's in Greenwich Village. In 1939, he joined Paul

Founder of the "Manhattan Guitar Club" for New York City session players, Art Ryerson was a highly regarded player before he left Ohio. *LFTJ.*

Whiteman as guitarist and arranger, having acquired a reputation for his innovative work with multiple guitars. A year or two later, he was a featured soloist with the great Raymond Scott Orchestra.

During World War II, Ryerson was assigned to the Thirty-fourth Special Services as a bandleader, performing for the troops in England, Belgium and France. Back in New York, he resumed working as a session player. In addition to playing on thousands of radio and TV broadcasts, he recorded with Bill Haley, Elvis Presley, Frank Sinatra, Tony Bennett, Peggy Lee, Red Norvo, Fats Waller, Charlie Parker, Ella Fitzgerald, Errol Garner, Lionel Hampton, Artie Shaw, Mildred Bailey and Anita O'Day. Ryerson was the first person to play electric guitar in an opera, mimicking a zither for Kurt Weill's *Rise and Fall of the City of Mahogany* at the Metropolitan Opera. In 1975, he took part in Louis Armstrong's Commemorative Tour to Russia.

THE SCOTT BROTHERS—BIG NOISE OUT OF SPRINGFIELD: CECIL XAVIER (1905–1964) AND LLOYD (1902–UNKNOWN)

As teenagers in Springfield, clarinet and sax player Cecil Scott and his brother Lloyd, a drummer, formed a trio with pianist Don Frye. By 1922, it had grown to a seven-piece ensemble, Scott's Symphonic Syncopators.

George Luggi (trombone), Art Hodes (piano) and Cecil Scott (clarinet) at Ole South, New York City, 1946. *WG-LOC.*

Two years later, the band ventured to New York for the first time, eventually becoming the resident group at the Savoy Ballroom in 1928. Although recordings were issued under both their names, Lloyd soon left the music making to Cecil and took over managing the group. Rechristened Cecil Scott's Bright Boys, the band included such sidemen as Joe Thomas, Johnny Hodges, Dickey Wells, Roy Eldridge and Leon "Chu" Berry.

When Cecil was seriously injured in an accident, resulting in the amputation of his leg, he had to quit playing for a year or two. Following his recovery, he joined the bands of Ellsworth Reynolds, Teddy Hill, Teddy Wilson and Billie Holiday. Known as one of the most driving and creative first-generation saxophonists, he entered the studio with Willie "the Lion" Smith, Henry "Red" Allen and Clarence Williams. In 1942, he put together his own combo, which included "Hot Lips" Page and Art Hodes. However, he disbanded the group in 1950 to join Jimmy McPartland. In all, Cecil Scott is credited with having played on at least seventy-five albums.

"LITTLE" JIMMY SCOTT: TOO PAINFUL FOR MOST LISTENERS TO TAKE (1925–   )

One of the most incredible stories in all of music is that of Little Jimmy Scott. Born with a rare genetic disorder that prevented him from experiencing puberty, Scott is a male contralto. Growing up in a series of foster homes and orphanages in Cleveland, he had a tough way to go until he was discovered by Lionel Hampton. Among his admirers were Billie Holiday, Charlie "Bird" Parker and Ray Charles, and he is cited as a major influence by Nancy Wilson, Marvin Gaye and Frankie Valli (who said that Scott's singing is too painful for most listeners to take).

Despite numerous setbacks, Scott's unfailing optimism enabled him "to work through the bad stuff." After three decades of neglect, he was rediscovered when he was in his late sixties. Signed to Sire Records, he found himself joining Lou Reed, Bruce Springsteen and Madonna on various projects. Scott is now regarded as quite possibly the greatest jazz singer of all time. "They say I don't belong in any category, male or female, pop or jazz," Scott said. "But early on, I saw my suffering as my salvation. Once I knew that, I understood that God had put me in this strange little package for a reason."

"Little" Jimmy Scott is better known in the autumn of his career than he was in his prime, due to new recordings and numerous re-releases such as this one on Rhino. *Rhino Records.*

CLIFFORD EVERETT "BUD" SHANK JR.: MR. WEST COAST COOL (1926–2009)

Born in Dayton, Bud Shank grew up on a farm. He started playing the clarinet at age ten, switching to tenor sax a couple years later. In 1944, he left home to attend the University of North Carolina, majoring in music and learning to play the flute. However, he quit school to go on the road. When the band broke up almost immediately, Shank moved to the West Coast, where he worked with Charlie Barnett, Alvino Rey, Art Mooney and Stan Kenton (1947–1951). He then joined Howard Rumsey's Lighthouse All-Stars (1953–56) and began making albums under his own name.

Shank wrote the music for several Bruce Brown surfing documentaries. An early proponent of world music, he recorded an album with Japanese kotoist Kimio Eto (1961) and with Indian sitarist Ravi Shankar (1962). In 1974, he was a founding member of the Brazilian-influenced LA 4. During the mid-1980s, he toured Europe as a soloist with former Kenton band mate Shorty Rogers. Although Shank is best known to the general public for his flute solos on the Mamas and the Papas' "California Dreamin'" (1965) and the Association's "Windy" (1967), music historians recognize him as one of the pioneering figures in the West Coast "cool jazz" movement.

THE SMITH BROTHERS—THE RIPLEY WONDERS: RUSSELL "POPS" (1890–1966) AND JOE SMITH (1902–1937)

Trumpeter Russell "Pops" Smith was taught music at the age of fourteen by his father in his hometown of Ripley, along with his younger brother, Joe. His first professional work was with the Six Music Spillers in 1910. Four years later, Pops traveled to Europe with the Joe Jordan Band before enlisting in the army. After demobilization, he joined the James Reese Europe civilian band (1919). In 1925, Pops became the lead trumpet in Fletcher Henderson's Orchestra and stayed with the group until 1942. Tenor player Ben Webster credits Pops with making him "tone-conscious." Jumping to Cab Calloway's band, he remained with that group until 1945. He then toured with the Noble Sissle Orchestra until 1950 before retiring from music.

"I used to hate him when he came in," Roy Eldridge recalled of trumpet player Joe Smith, "because otherwise I had the joint locked up!" A wild man in comparison to his brother Russell, Joe was known for his plunger-mute style, which emulated a crooning human voice. By his late teens, Smith was a working musician in New York City, accompanying Ethel Waters and Mamie Smith. In 1924, Sissle and Blake had hired him as music director for their latest production, *In Bamville*. Using a coconut mute, he appeared onstage at the conclusion of each show to play the "walking-out music." Hired by Fletcher Henderson (1925–28) and then McKinney's Cotton Pickers (1929–30), he accidentally killed his friend, vocalist George "Fathead" Thomas, in an automobile accident when both were drunk. Although he later worked with several name bands, he proved unstable. Finally, in 1933, Joe was found incoherent in Kansas City. He spent the remaining four years of his life in a New York sanitarium.

Hezekiah Leroy Gordon "Stuff" Smith: Jazz Violin Pioneer (1909–1967)

The Smiths were a very musical family; the mother played piano and the father, violin. Young "Stuff," born in Portsmouth and reared in Massillon and Cleveland, was also playing violin by the age of six. His musical abilities won him a scholarship to the Johnson C. Smith University, where, at age fifteen, he quit school and joined a musical revue. It was during this time that he gained his nickname. From 1926 to 1930, he played with Alphonso Trent in Texas before moving to New York to form his own quintet. Smith began playing an amplified violin, the first person to do so. Signed to the Vocalion label, he immediately scored a hit with "I'se a Muggin" (1936).

Two years later, Smith participated in the first outdoor jazz festival, the Carnival of Swing on New York's Randall's Island. In 1943, while a member of Fats Waller's Band, Smith was chosen to take over when Waller

One of the true pioneers of the jazz violin, Hezekiah "Stuff" Smith, whose influence is still felt. *DS.*

died. He eventually settled in Copenhagen, where he continued to play and record. Over the years, Smith performed with everyone from Coleman Hawkins and Dizzy Gillespie to Charlie Parker and Sun Ra. Along with Joe Venuti and Stephane Grappelli, he is considered one of the greatest and most influential swing violinists.

MAMIE ROBINSON SMITH: THE QUEEN OF THE BLUES (1883–1946)

Born Mamie Robinson in Cincinnati, vocalist Mamie Smith occupies a significant place in music history as the first African American woman to make a non-gospel recording. On February 14, 1920, she recorded "That Thing Called Love" and "You Can't Keep a Good Man Down" on the Okeh label as a last-minute replacement for Sophie Tucker. Six months later, on August 19, she returned to the studio to cut several more songs, including "Crazy Blues"—the first blues vocal by a black artist. It sold more than one million copies in less than a year.

Billed as the "Queen of the Blues," Smith opened the door for others of her race, and by the end of 1923, no fewer than nine other record

All the blues singers who came afterward are indebted to the woman who started it all, "Queen of the Blues" Mamie Smith. *DS.*

companies had similar artists. The thirty-six-year-old Smith was a veteran vaudeville and nightclub performer who possessed a lively stage personality, and with her lavish costumes and fancy jewelry, she set the style for "divas" who followed. She continued to perform and record with her band, the Jazz Hounds (which included Coleman Hawkins), and appeared in several films, including *Paradise in Harlem* (1939). However, she was quickly overshadowed by Bessie Smith, eleven years her junior, who took the title "Empress of the Blues."

SAMMY STEWART: PIONEER OF SYMPHONIC JAZZ (1890–1960)

Pianist, organist and bandleader Sammy Stewart was born in Circleville and got his start in Columbus as a member of Parker's Popular Players. In 1918, he broke away from Parker to form Sammy Stewart and His Singing Syncopators (later the Ten Knights of Syncopation), which was one of the first territory bands. The group was so successful with its "symphonic jazz" music

In his pre-Chicago days, Sammy Stewart's Singing Syncopators included Harley Washington, Frank Fowler, Earl Hood, Dave Smallwood, Andrew Henick, Sammy Stewart, Grant Williams and Claudius Forney. *LFTJ.*

that in 1923 the Sammy Stewart Orchestra became the featured attraction at Chicago's Sunset Café and later the Savoy and Arcadia Ballrooms in New York City. Stewart had his pick of the best players available, including drummer Sid Catlett and tenor saxophonist Leon "Chu" Berry. However, a young Louis Armstrong failed his audition.

When the musicians' union in New York insisted Stewart replace half his band with local players, he quit the band business. Instead, he became a keyboard soloist, working the best hotels and nightclubs. As his protégé, Earl Hood, recalled, "He was the first man I ever saw who could play two melodies simultaneously; one in one hand and another in the other." For many years, Hood used his mentor's arrangements for his own band. In his declining years, Stewart supported himself by giving music lessons in his New York apartment.

WILLIAM "BILLY" STRAYHORN: A NEARLY INVISIBLE GENIUS (1915–1967)

The man who lived in Ellington's shadow, Billy Strayhorn, photographed in New York City, circa 1946–48. *WG-LOC.*

Pianist, composer and arranger Billy Strayhorn was born in Dayton but moved with his family to Pittsburgh, Pennsylvania. He received musical training as a youth and briefly played the piano in Mercer Ellington's band in 1938, when he met Duke Ellington, Mercer's father. Within the year, Strayhorn joined the elder Ellington's band as a lyric writer and second pianist. Ellington was so impressed with the young man's talent that he soon recorded "Something to Live For." Before a year had passed, Strayhorn began arranging and composing for Ellington. This was the beginning of a lifelong collaboration lasting until Strayhorn's death twenty-eight years later.

So close was the partnership between Ellington and Strayhorn that it is difficult to say where one stopped and the other began. Strayhorn lived and worked in the Duke's shadow, a fact Ellington acknowledged when he said, "Strayhorn does a lot of the work, but I get to take the bows." Sometimes he was given credit, sometimes he shared it and sometimes he was overlooked. However, Strayhorn is known to have composed "Lush Life" (1938), "Something to Live For" (1939), "Take the A Train" (1941) and "Chelsea Bridge" (1941) and to have contributed to many other pieces. Scott Yanow called him "a nearly invisible genius."

Arthur "Art" Tatum: God Has Just Come into the Room (1910–1956)

"Ladies and Gentlemen, God has just come into the room," pianist Fats Waller once announced as Art Tatum entered a club where he was playing. Born in Toledo, he attended the Ohio School for the Blind and the Toledo School of Music. He could play violin, accordion and, especially, piano.

"In my entire career as a photographer," Herman Leonard said, "only two subjects made me tremble with fear and excitement...Albert Einstein and Art Tatum [pictured], because I knew I was in the presence of, and in private, privileged contact with, true geniuses." *©Herman Leonard Photography LLC.*

While still in his teens, he began playing around his hometown, making his professional debut on WSPD radio. Before he was twenty, Tatum had worked with Speed Webb. Moving to New York City, he went on tour with Adelle Hall (1932) and then returned to the Midwest, where he worked mainly in Cleveland before relocating to Chicago.

In 1943, Tatum formed a trio with Tiny Grimes and Slam Stewart. From then on, he divided his time between trio and solo work, nightclub and concert appearances in Toronto, New York, Chicago and Hollywood. In 1944, he performed at the Metropolitan Opera House and had a cameo in the film *The Fabulous Dorseys* (1947). According to *Jazz Rough Guide*, "Like no other performer in the history of jazz piano, Art Tatum summarized everything that had preceded him stylistically and did it with a supercharged manner that opened doors, not only for succeeding generations of pianists but for other performers as well."

CHARLES PHILLIP "SIR CHARLES" THOMPSON: A STRANGE CAT (1918–)

Sir Charles at the organ, with Rudy Powell on sax, at Count Basie's Bar in Harlem during the early 1950s. *DS.*

Self-knighted "Sir" Charles Thompson first studied violin but traded it for the piano while still a youth in Springfield. At age fifteen, he left home to join the Lloyd Hunter Orchestra in Nebraska. By the late 1930s, he was playing with Midwest territory bands, including the Nate Towles Orchestra. During 1940–41, he worked with Lionel Hampton, leaving to play in a smaller group led by Lester Young in New York City. He also began contributing arrangements to Jimmy Dorsey, Fletcher Henderson, Count Basie and others. Thompson remained in New York and played with Don Byas, Hot

Lips Page and Roy Eldridge. However, from 1944 to 1945, Thompson was accompanying Coleman Hawkins out in California.

Clearly influenced by Count Basie (both in name and piano style), Thompson was able to make the transition from swing to bop. While playing with Illinois Jacquet in 1947, he composed the bop classic, "Robbin's Nest," which became Jacquet's biggest hit record and a jazz standard. In addition to freelancing as an organist, he recorded his own small group albums for Vanguard and Columbia in the 1950s. Once described by Miles Davis as "a strange cat," Thompson continued to write and record numerous albums and tour all over the world into his eighties.

Norris William Turney: The Duke's Flute Player (1921–2001)

Wilmington's Norris Turney was an accomplished saxophone, clarinet and flute player. He initially worked with A.B. Townsend's band, followed by a tour with the Jeter-Pillars Orchestra. In 1945, he joined the Tiny Bradshaw Orchestra in Chicago and the same year went to New York to play and

An Andy Snow publicity shot for the late Norris Turney, whom Duke Ellington hired as an "insurance policy" for the ailing Johnny Hodges. *LFTJ.*

record with Billy Eckstine. After a stint with Elmer Snowden in 1951, Turney returned to Ohio to play in various local groups. He joined Ray Charles in 1967 for a tour of Australia before becoming a full-time member of the Duke Ellington Orchestra (1969–73).

Initially, Turney was to sub for the ailing Johnny Hodges (for whom he wrote "Checkered Hat"), but soon he was also Ellington's first flute soloist on "Bourbon Street Jingling Jollies." After leaving Ellington, he settled down in New York City, where he worked in various Broadway theater orchestras when not leading his own ensemble (1975–78). Having gained a reputation as one of the most lyrical alto players on the scene, he was featured in both Frank Foster and Clark Terry's groups. Then, during the 1980s, he joined Panama Francis's Savoy Sultans and George Wein's Newport All-Stars, with whom he toured internationally. Turney continued to work and record up through his final years.

JOHN J. ULRICH: NOBODY'S AS GOOD AS JOHNNY (1922–2008)

For seventy-two years, John Ulrich earned a living as a pianist, teacher and arranger. Born in Pennsylvania, he began playing professionally at age twelve. In addition to the piano, he played vibraphone and trumpet. Ulrich came to

John Ulrich could never pass a piano without stopping to play a few songs. *LFTJ*.

Columbus to earn a degree in music education at Capital University. Among the many musicians he worked with over the years were George Towne, Muggsy Spanier, Don Goldie, Roy Liberto, Walter "Pee Wee" Hunt and Dick Baars. He joined Phil Napoleon in Miami, Jack Maheu in Salt Lake City and New York City and spent a year or two on the road with Wild Bill Davison before touring with Bobby Hackett.

During the 1970s, Ulrich often played with Smoky Stover and Gene Mayl's

Rhythm Kings. A popular performer on the festival circuit, he also served on the jazz faculty at Denison and Capital Universities. When Terry Waldo moved to New York City, he found there were a lot of good piano players, but none of them was as good as Johnny Ulrich. Ulrich was a master of the stride style, as his recordings demonstrate. That he is not better known is due to the simple fact that he preferred to live a simple life, close to his family.

EUGENE "GENE" WALKER: ON TOUR WITH THE BEATLES (1938–   )

In 1956, reedman Gene Walker left his home in Columbus to go on his first professional tour. Since then, he has worked with the likes of King Curtis, Jackie Wilson, Sam Cooke, Chris Columbo, Johnny "Hammond" Smith and Jimmy McGriff. In addition to performing with the King Curtis Band on the 1965 Beatles tour, he has played at Carnegie Hall, the Saratoga (New York) Jazz Festival, the North Sea Jazz Festival (Holland) and the Umbria Jazz Festival (Italy). For a number of years, Walker worked as a studio musician in New York City on sessions for Lloyd Price, Archie "Stomp" Gordon, Byrdie Green, Chris Columbo and Freddie McCoy (playing a Selmer Electronic Varitone sax!).

From Cannibal and the Headhunters to Jack McDuff, Gene Walker has had a long and varied career, both as a session player and a performer. *LFTJ.*

Walker received a degree in music from Ohio State University in 1988. He then joined the school's faculty, teaching saxophone improvisation and combo classes, along with jazz history at the OSU Jazz Ensemble Camp and at the Jamey Abersold Summer Workshops. During 1986 and 1987, renowned guitarist Eric Gale traveled from New York each week to play in Walker's Columbus band. Walker's work is rooted in the deepest traditions of jazz, and he is dedicated to perpetuating the art form through education and performance. Artistic director for the Listen for the Jazz project, he also leads his Cotton Club Orchestra and Generations Band.

EARLE WARREN:
THE COUNT'S MAN AND THE COUNTSMEN (1914–1994)

Originally from Springfield, Earle Warren started out on piano before switching to reeds. After high school graduation, he moved his band, Duke Warren and His Eight Counts of Syncopation, to Columbus before joining

After singing and playing with the original Count Basie Orchestra in the 1930s, Earle Warren spent many years in Europe. *WG-LOC.*

the Marion Sears Orchestra in Cleveland. Warren soon discovered that Art Tatum was playing in a nearby club and would join him after his gigs to sing for tips, which he split with the piano player. In 1936, he became the primary alto saxophonist for the original Count Basie Orchestra, remaining with it off and on through the end of the 1940s. During this time, Warren directed the Basie Orchestra on some recordings that were released by the Earle Warren Orchestra.

Warren once recalled how the Basie band had proclaimed itself as the finest swing band in the land, and when he came off the bandstand he would be "wringing wet" from blowing so hard. When Basie was happy with the tempo he had established, he would call out, "That's it!" and Warren would pick it up to lead the sax section. Around 1970, Warren formed the Countsmen, a sextet built around Basie's musicians such as trombonist Dickey Wells and bassist Peck Morrison. After eleven years, he moved to Switzerland but continued to perform with the band, primarily in New York City.

OLIVER HAYDEN "JIGGS" WHIGHAM III: PROFESSOR FOR LIFE (1943–   )

An American jazz trombonist who lives in Europe, Jiggs Whigham was born in Cleveland and began playing professionally at the age of seventeen in the Glenn Miller Orchestra. Two years later, he toured with Stan Kenton's "mellophonium"[59] band before settling in New York City. Unhappy with the scene there, he moved to Germany. Since then, he has played in the bands of Kurt Edelhagen, Bert Kaempfert and Peter Herbolzheimer and has made many recordings as a leader. He has also been the musical director of Germany's Radio-In-The-American Sector (RIAS) Big Band, Britain's BBC Big Band and the Berlin Jazz Orchestra.

Over the years, Whigham has worked with Bill Holman, Niels-Henning Ørsted Pedersen and Carl Fontana. In 1979, he was named head of the Jazz Department at the Cologne University College of Music, the first appointment of its kind in Germany. Sixteen years later, he was named "Professor for Life" at the Hanns Eisler College of Music in Berlin. He also is "artist-in-residence" for Conn-Selmer, maker of the King-Jiggs Whigham trombone. Recently, he has been promoting the Jiggs P-Bone, a trombone made entirely of plastic. When not traveling the world as a soloist, conductor and educator, Whigham divides his time between homes in Germany and the United States.

ZACK WHYTE:
A TOP TERRITORY BAND LEADER (1898–1967)

Although Zack Whyte hailed from Kentucky, he played an important part in Ohio jazz history from 1922 to 1937 as leader of one of the top territory bands, the Cincinnati-based Zack Whyte and His Chocolate Beau Brummels. Whyte originally came to the Buckeye State to attend Wilberforce College, where he played banjo in Horace Henderson's Collegians. He also contributed arrangements to the group. After briefly joining Fletcher Henderson's ensemble, he realized there was money to be made in the band business.

About 1923 or 1924, Whyte formed the Chocolate Beau Brummels, which included Vic Dickenson, Eugene "Sy" Oliver, Quentin Jackson, Herman Chittison, Al Sears, Roy Eldridge and many other first-rate musicians. In 1929, Whyte and his band made some recordings for Gennett Studios in Richmond, Indiana, which also appeared on the Supertone and

Zack Whyte and his Orchestra, circa 1931. *From left to right*: Zack Whyte (leader), William "Billy" King (piano), William Benton (drums), Madison "Rockin' Chair" Lennone (bass), Mr. Alexander (banjo), Earl "Inky" Tribble (sax), Sy Oliver (trumpet), Steve Dunn (trumpet), Fred Jackson (sax), Vic Dickenson (trombone) and Clarence Paige (sax). *DS.*

Champion labels. Some of these were released under the names Eddie Walker and His Band and Smoke Jackson and His Red Onions. The group's most popular song was "Mandy." However, the Beau Brummels ("a bunch of idiots," in Oliver's opinion) constantly fought over how to play. In self-defense, Oliver started writing arrangements for the band in what would later be called the "Jimmie Lunceford sound," ushering in the swing era. By 1939, Whyte had retired.

Nancy Wilson:
The Voice Was Always a Part of Me (1937–   )

Singer Nancy Wilson was born in Chillicothe but lived in Columbus from the age of four. "I sang at school, in church, at home, anywhere I could," Wilson recalled. "The voice was always a part of me." In 1947, she heard Little Jimmy Scott and began to pattern her singing style after

The legendary Nancy Wilson, winner of the 2004 National Endowment for the Arts (NEA) Jazz Masters Fellowships award. *LFTJ.*

his. While still in her teens, Nancy hosted her own TV show, *Skyline Melodies*. The night of her high school prom, she met Rusty Bryant, who offered her a job the next day, but she decided she wasn't ready. She subsequently dropped out of Central State College after a semester to join him on the road.

While with Bryant, Wilson met Julian "Cannonball" Adderley, who told her to look him up if she ever came to New York. In 1962, she did just that, and his manager, John Levy, quickly got her a contract with Capital Records. Her second single, "(You Don't Know) How Glad I Am," reached number eleven in 1964. In partnership with Levy, Wilson became a star of the first order, recording more than sixty albums, winning three Grammys, starring on radio and TV and receiving innumerable honors. In 1998, she won the Playboy Reader Poll Award for best jazz vocalist. She was inducted into the International Civil Rights Walk of Fame in 2005.

MITCHELL W. "BOOTIE" WOOD: BOOTIE'S BLUES (1919–1987)

Bootie Wood took time off to deliver the mail between working with Count Basie and Duke Ellington. *Cityfolk Archives.*

Trombonist Bootie (or "Booty") Wood studied music while attending Dunbar High School in Dayton. Following graduation, he and a friend, trumpeter Eugene "Snooky" Young, went on the road with the Chick Carter Band (1938–39). During the 1940s, Wood played in the bands of Tiny Bradshaw, Lionel Hampton, Arnett Cobb and Erskine Hawkins. A technically accomplished player, Wood was a strong sideman who took advantage of his few opportunities to solo, but the big band era was ending.

Following six months with Count Basie, Wood returned to Dayton in 1951 to take a job with the U.S. Post Office. He also was a member of Snooky Young's band, along with bassist Slam Stewart. In 1959, Wood rejoined the Count Basie Orchestra, where he remained until 1963. During this period, he occasionally recorded with Duke Ellington. In 1968, he toured Europe with the Earl Hines band. Three years later, Wood joined his old buddies Snooky Young and Norris Turney for the album *The Boys from Dayton*, which highlighted the mother lode of talent to come from that area. He also went back on the road with Basie, recording "Bootie's Blues" (1979). As late as 1981, he appeared with the Basie Orchestra on a Sarah Vaughn album.

Eugene Edward "Snooky" Young: Mr. Dependable (1919–2011)

Dayton's Snooky Young first played the zither before switching to the trumpet as a member of his family's touring band. He also worked in the bands of Eddie Heywood Sr. and Graham Jackson in Atlanta, Georgia, before returning home to finish high school. As a student at Wilberforce College, he played with the Collegians. Then, during the 1930s, Young spent time in the bands of Jimmie Lunceford, Count Basie, Lionel Hampton, Les Hite and Chick Carter. Remaining loyal to Count Basie and Lionel Hampton, he played only short stints with Benny Carter and others throughout the 1940s.

Young appeared in several films in the 1940s, most notably *Blues in the Night* (1941), in which he played the trumpet solo for actor Jack Carson's character. Returning to Dayton, he led his own band when not on the road. From 1956 to 1962, he returned to Basie and then left to freelance in New York City, where he worked with Charles Mingus and became the studio trumpeter for NBC. He was a founding member of the Thad Jones–Mel Lewis Orchestra (1966–72), before moving to Los Angeles, where he frequently performed in the *Tonight Show* Orchestra. Trumpeter Buck Clayton said Young was "one of the most dependable trumpet players in the business."

Smoking may have been prohibited on the premises, but that didn't stop Mory Feld from "smokin'" behind his drum kit. *WG-LOC.*

Notes

Introduction

1. "The Origins of Jazz," http://www.redhotjazz.com/originsarticle.html.
2. Berendt and Huesmann, *Jazz Book*.
3, Osborne, *Music in Ohio*.
4. Edison and Byrne only learned about this connection when they sat together at the Columbus Senior Musicians Hall of Fame induction ceremony a month before Edison passed away. It was the first time they had seen each other in thirty-one years.
5. An aside to Vaughn Wiester, who once said, "I want the book that has Phil Sunkel in it." This is it.
6. Geoffrey Himes, "Von Freeman and the Case for Jazz's Hometown Heroes," *http://www.npr.org/blogs/ablogsupreme/2011/07/17/138174554/von-freeman-and-the-case-for-jazzs-hometown-heroes* (accessed July 15, 2011).

Chapter 1

7. Native American music seldom comes up in these conversations.
8. McCarthy, *Big Band Jazz*.
9. http://parlorsongs.com/insearch/ragtime/ragtime.php.
10. Abbott and Seroff., *Ragged But Right*.
11. Jasen and Jones, *Spreadin' Rhythm Around*.
12. *Record Changer*, December, 1947
13. Jasen, *Ragtime*.

14. Neddermeyer was a prolific composer of marches, waltzes, two-steps, popular songs and, reportedly, at least one opera, but few have survived.
15. sitemaker.umich.edu/GVCSiteMaker/Styles/.../Cincinnati.doc.
16. David Thomas Roberts's liner notes to *The Amazon Rag* (Stomp Off Records, 1985).
17. Jelly Roll Morton felt that Matthews was the best piano player in St. Louis.
18. Ohio, not Delaware, as some sources have reported.
19. Published in the *Miami Conservancy Bulletin*.

CHAPTER 2

20. Maym Kelso's Edison cylinder "Because" (1899) may have been the earliest recording by an Ohioan. She was an actress and vaudeville performer who sang ballads and minstrel songs, sometimes in a "Negro" dialect.
21. By 1911, Sweatman was playing three clarinets simultaneously in his vaudeville act.
22. Hennessey, *Jazz to Swing*.
23. Watkins, *Showman*.
24. Gushee, *Pioneers of Jazz*.
25. *Edison Amberola Monthly* (August, 1918).
26. Heining, *George Russell*.

CHAPTER 3

27. Keller, *Dance and Its Music in America*.
28. Berlin, *King of Ragtime*.
29. Arthur Murray claims to be the second-oldest franchised business of any kind behind A&W Restaurants, which began franchising in 1921.
30. Golden, *Vernon and Irene Castle's Ragtime Revolution*.
31. While it was rumored that Bix Beiderbecke played on the session, the cornetist was actually Ohio State student Leroy Morris.

Chapter 4

32. *Music Trades*, December 2, 1922

33. http://pressf1.pcworld.co.nz/showthread.php?45825-Off-Topic-HTOTW-19-Ted-Weems-and-his-Orchestra.

34. In 1935, McCoy co-founded *DownBeat*, the music magazine.

Chapter 5

35. Simon, *Big Bands*.

36. Even Marie Behm got into the business in a small way, playing piano in the four-piece S.O.S. Orchestra.

37. Dahl, *Stormy Weather*.

38. Tucker, *Swing Shift*.

Chapter 6

39. Crowther and Pinfold, *Singing Jazz*.

40. Friedwald, *Biographical Guide*.

41. Sadly, Black had died seven years earlier.

42. While Louis Armstrong is often given credit for being the first scat singer, many ragtime songs included meaningless, rhythmic syllables in the lyrics (like many folk songs going back as far as Shakespeare's time).

43. Sissle graduated from high school in Cleveland, where he sang in several choirs.

44. Berendt and Huesmann, *Jazz Book*. .

Chapter 7

45. *Jazz Pedagogy*, 1979.

46. Also in Columbus, the all-girl Johnny Cheuvront Orchestra was assembled by John W. Cheuvront (1904–1993), a forty-year-old painter and sometime bandleader.

47. Francis and Caso, *Tuskegee Airmen*.

48. Joe Mosbrook, *Jazzed in Cleveland: Part Twenty-Eight* (WMV Web News Cleveland series, August 29, 1997).

CHAPTER 8

49. Rose, *I Remember Jazz*.

CHAPTER 9

50. In the late 1950s, Rogers set the world record for marathon drumming in the window of Ziggy Coyle's Music Store: eighty hours, thirty-five minutes and fourteen seconds, beating out an average of sixty-five strokes a minute.
51. The normaphone is a valve trombone shaped like an alto sax.

CHAPTER 10

52. Trombonist Jim Gary's first encounter with him was during a jam session in the 1950s, when Kirk suddenly blew a police whistle in his ear.
53. Kirk plays flute on the album under the pseudonym Theoshis Tannis.

CHAPTER 11

54. Providing steady employment for many Ohio musicians.

CHAPTER 12

55. Byron Rooker substituted for Bryant due to a prior commitment.
56. It is the oldest such organization in the United States, founded fifteen years before the Jazz at Lincoln Center Orchestra.

CHAPTER 13

57. It's not always easy to identify Ohio musicians. Vocalist and pianist Billie Walker studied at Artie Matthews's school and with one of the instructors at the College-Conservatory. However, when he was hired to play New York, his agent cautioned him, "Don't tell anyone you're from Cincinnati. Say you're from Detroit."

58. In *The Big Bands*, George T. Simon listed the top personnel of the leading big bands of 1938. It is interesting to note the number of Buckeyes who appear in the ranks. Count Basi had Earle Warren (Springfield) on alto sax and Harry "Sweets" Edison (Columbus) on trumpet. Bob Crosby had Billy Butterfield (Middletown) on trumpet and Marion Mann (Columbus) on vocals. Jimmy Dorsey had Bobby Byrne (Pleasant Corners) on trombone. Glen Gray had Walter "Pee Wee" Hunt (Mount Healthy/Columbus) on trombone and vocals. Horace Heidt had Frank DeVol (Canton) on sax and Alvino Rey (Cleveland) on guitar. Jimmie Lunceford had Joe Thomas (all over Ohio) on sax and Sy Oliver (Zanesville) on trumpet. Paul Whiteman had Roy Bargy (Toledo) on piano and Art Ryerson (Columbus) on guitar. These musicians were stars in their respective groups.

59. A trumpet-like substitute for the French horn.

Selected Bibliography

As trite as it may sound, the authors have barely scratched the surface (the original manuscript was twice as long). If you want to learn more about jazz in Ohio, we invite you to start with these sources and just keep going.

Abbot, Lynn, and Doug Seroff. *Ragged But Right: Black Traveling Shows, "Coon Songs," and the Dark Pathway to Blues and Jazz*. Jackson: University Press of Mississippi, 2007.

Bauer, Bishop, Einhorn, Howard, Johnson, Lentz, Lynch, Marr, McDaniel, Meyers, Prillerman, Smith, Stan, Walker and Watkins. *Listen for the Jazz: Keynotes in Columbus History*. Columbus, OH: Arts Foundation of Olde Towne, 1990, 1992.

Berendt, Joachim-Ernst, and Gunther Huesmann. *The Jazz Book: From Ragtime to the 21ˢᵗ Century*. Chicago, IL: Lawrence Hill Books, 2009.

Berlin, Edward A. *King of Ragtime: Scott Joplin and His Era*. New York: Viking, 1994.

Blesh, Rudi, and Harriett Janis. *They All Played Ragtime: The True Story of an American Music*. New York: Alfred A. Knopf, 1950.

Claghorn, Charles E. *Biographical Dictionary of Jazz*. Englewood Cliffs, NJ: Prentice Hall, 1982.

Crowther, Bruce, and Mike Pinfold. *Singing Jazz: The Singers and Their Styles*. N.p.: Backbeat Books, 1998.

Dahl, Linda. *Stormy Weather: The Music and Lives of a Century of Jazz Women*. New York: Limelight Editions, 1989.

Dance, Stanley. *The World of Swing: An Oral History of Big Band Jazz.* Cambridge, MA: Da Capo Press, 2001.

Feather, Leonard. *The Encyclopedia of Jazz.* New York: Bonanza Books, 1960.

———. *The Encyclopedia of Jazz in the Seventies.* New York: Horizon Press, 1977.

———. *The Encyclopedia of Jazz in the Sixties.* New York: Bonanza Books, 1966.

Francis, Charles E., and Adolph Caso. *The Tuskegee Airmen: The Men Who Changed a Nation.* Wellesley, MA: Branden Books, 1999.

Friedwald, Will. *A Biographical Guide to the Great Jazz and Pop Singers.* New York: Pantheon Books, 2010.

Golden, Eve. *Vernon and Irene Castle's Ragtime Revolution.* Lexington: University Press of Kentucky, 2007.

Gushee, Lawrence. *Pioneers of Jazz: The Story of the Creole Band.* New York: Oxford University Press, 2001.

Heining, Duncan. *George Russell: The Story of an American Composer.* Lanham, MD: Scarecrow Press, 2009.

Hennessey, Thomas J. *Jazz to Swing: African American Jazz Musicians and Their Music, 1890–1935.* Detroit, MI: Wayne State University Press, 1994.

Jasen, David A. *Ragtime: An Encyclopedia, Discography, and Sheetography.* New York: Routledge, 2007.

Jasen, David A., and Gene Jones. *Spreadin' Rhythm Around.* New York: Schirmer Books, 1998.

Keller, Kate Van Winkle. *Dance and Its Music in America, 1528–1789.* 2007. Hillsdale, NY: Pendragon Press, 2007.

McCarthy, Albert. *Big Band Jazz.* New York: Exeter Books, 1983.

McNutt, Randy. *King Records of Cincinnati.* Charleston, SC: Arcadia Publishing, 2009.

Meyers, David, Arnett Howard, James Loeffler and Candice Watkins. *Columbus, The Musical Crossroads.* Charleston, SC: Arcadia Publishing, 2008.

Mosbrook, Joe. *Cleveland Jazz History.* Cleveland, OH: Northeast Ohio Jazz Society, Inc., 2003.

Osborne, William. *Music in Ohio.* Kent, OH: Kent State University Press, 2004.

Reese, Greg L., and Rodney L. Brown. *Jazzkeepers: A Pictorial Tribute and Memoir.* Cleveland, OH: Four-G Publishers, 1996.

Rose, Al. *I Remember Jazz: Six Decades Among the Great Jazzmen.* Baton Rouge: Louisiana State University Press, 1987.

Simon, George T. *The Big Bands.* London: MacMillan, 1967.

Tucker, Sherri. *Swing Shift: "All-Girl" Bands of the 1940s.* Durham, NC: Duke University Press, 2000.

Waldo, Terry. *This Is Ragtime.* New York: Hawthorn Books, 1976.

Walker, Leo. *The Big Band Almanac.* Rev. ed. New York: Da Capo, 1989.

Watkins, Clifford E. *Showman: The Life and Music of Perry George Lowery.* Jackson: University Press of Mississippi, 2003.

Index

About the Authors

The authors of *Ohio Jazz: A History of Jazz in the Buckeye State* previously collaborated on *Columbus, The Musical Crossroads* (Arcadia, 2008) and *Listen for the Jazz: Key Notes in Columbus History* (Arts Foundation of Olde Towne, 1990–92).

DAVID MEYERS has spent nearly thirty years documenting the history of music in central Ohio and was formerly host of *Bring 'Em Back Alive*, a weekly radio program on local music history.

An artist and community activist, CANDICE WATKINS is a driving force behind two of the city's largest annual music festivals: Hot Times and ComFest.

ARNETT HOWARD, arguably the best-known musician in Columbus, has devoted much of the past three decades to interviewing many of the pioneering jazz musicians in the community.

The authors (clockwise from center): Candice Watkins, James Loeffler, Arnett Howard and David Meyers. *Larry Hamill Photography.*

And JAMES LOEFFLER, former publisher of the *Antique Review*, is a well-known collector of jazz recordings and is a board member and former president of the Central Ohio Hot Jazz Society.

Visit us at
www.historypress.net